JN121927

大学の喪失
その再生への期待
詩人ウェンデル・ベリーの教育論

ウェンデル・ベリー 著
鈴木順子・宗宮弘明 訳

風媒社

目次

訳者まえがき

鈴木順子

本書は、ウェンデル・ベリー著「大学の喪失　その再生への希望」(Wendell Berry, “The loss of the University”, in *Home Economics*, pp.76-97, North Point Press, 1987）の翻訳である。

著者のウェンデル・ベリー（1934- ）は、アメリカ社会における行き過ぎた新自由主義的傾向の資本主義に警鐘を鳴らし、本来の人間社会のあるべき姿がどのようなものかを、多くの著作を通して一貫して示し続けている作家、詩人、批評家である。彼が現在、アメリカ社会の現状に疑問を感じる人々から大きな信頼を寄せられ、その発言がよく参照される思想家の一人であることは言うをまたないのだが、その理由の一つに、著作を通じて読み取れる叡智に富んだ思想のみならず、彼がその生地アメリカ南部で農業を経営しつつ、環境活動家として積極的に活躍しているということがある。

今年89歳になるが、彼の人間や故郷に対する深い愛と、知的冷静さを併せ持ちながら、常に言動一致した生活をしているその生き方、存在のあり方に、米国のみならず世界中から尊敬が集まっている思想家、社会活動家なのである。日本では、坂本龍一監修『非戦』幻冬舎、2002年に彼の論が所収されて以後、その存在が知られるようになった。また、最近オバマ元大統領が年間ベストブックとして評価し全米ベストセラーになった本で、生産性至上主義に傾くアメリカ社会を批判したジェニー・オデル『何もしない』(2021年）という本があるのだが、その中にも、ウェンデル・ベリーへの敬意に満ちた言及、引用があるのを見つけた。現在の社会状況を憂い、鋭い問題提起を行う若い思想家たちにも、ベリーが大きな影響力を持っていることが垣間見える。

共訳者宗宮弘明氏を通じて、このウェンデル・ベリーという思想家に遅ればせながら出会った筆者は、本書の翻訳に先立ち、ベリーの他の著書『ライフ・イズ・ミラクル』『ウェンデル・ベリーの環境思想』を読む機会を得た。その時の感動は忘れられない。同時代人に、これほど深く現代文明の問題点について考え、広い視野に立って解決策を示し、そして何より自分の言論内容と生活とを一致させている思想家、社会活動家がいるということに深い感銘を受けた。また、自分が常日頃研究している、シモーヌ・ヴェイユというフランス人哲学者・社会活動家と相通じるところを多数発見した。

作者ウェンデル・ベリーについては、「あとがき」に詳しいのでそちらもご覧いただくとして、ここでは、ベリーの作品「大学の喪失」の読み方について共訳者として、また日頃から大学でリベラルアーツ教育に携わる者として一言申し上げたい。

本作品においては、ベリーの教育論が余すところなく展開されているが、特に、ベリーは、大学のあり方を批判的にかつ建設的な提案も含めて論じる。その際、想像力を大事にする人文知（ヒューマニティーズ）の重要性を強調し、人文知の上に立ってこそ、大学教育の未来が築けるとの見解を示している。

すなわち、この著作は一言で言えば、まさにリベラル・アーツに立脚した教育論、文明論になっている。確かに、この作品は今の大学が直面する危機についての分析・提言であるのだが、教育問題を大きく越え出て、現代文明全体の広い視野でこれらを取り上げているところにその特徴がある。この鋭く深い問題提起の書を、教員や大学生のみならず、広く教育に関心を持つ人に読んでいただきたいと思うゆえんである。

ただ、実際に訳を検討しながら感じたのは、彼の作品に対する好き、嫌いは読者によってはっきりと分かれるだろうということである。また、彼の発言のある部分は賛成するが他のある部分は到底受け入れ難い、といった感想をもつ読み手もいるかもしれない、ということである。特に、彼のキリスト教（どちらかといえば保守的とされる南部バプテスト連盟にいたことが知られている）的価値観への立脚や、共同体主義への傾倒、農業経済の提唱などについては、若干古風で理想を追いすぎているのではないかと感じる読者もいることだろう。

確かに、産業経済の発展も大事と考える読者もいるはずであるのに、ベリーにはそうした読者に対して、優しくわかりやすく説得するといった配慮や、現代の一般的価値観への妥協、中庸への気配りなどは一切しない。

しかし、おそらく、古今東西の優れた思想家は皆（ベリーであれ、ヴェイユであれ）その妥協をゆるさない言説の鋭さ、他に類を見ない個性の強さ、現実の認識の深さにおいて、人からの評価、好き嫌いはくっきりと分かれるものではないだろうか。むしろそのように同時代人からの評価や好き嫌いが分かれることこそ、偉大な思想家であることの証明であろう。

初めて読む時には、とりあえず丸ごと彼の主張を受け入れながら読んでいただきたい。本当に美味で体に良い食べ物は、噛み始めた瞬間にはわからなくても、後からじわじわと滋味が感じられ体に沁み渡ってくるものであろうし、それは、文章にも言えることである。私たちの知性や倫理観を確実に養ってくれる文章とは、こういうものに違いないと訳の作業を進めながら強く感じた。

先述の通り、ベリーの小説、詩、エッセイは現在多数出版されており、ネット上ではインタビューなども読むことができる。アメリカはもちろんのこと、世界中の環境と地球の未来を真剣に考える人々の中で、彼の作品、思想、生き方への共感は静かに広がりつつある。

今回、訳の進め方としては、宗宮氏がまず全体を訳し、その後鈴木が、さらに宗宮氏が、というように何度も訳稿を往復させ訂正、改訳を繰り返した。最後は、三島浩路先生（現代教育学部長、本書「解説」執筆者）、太田明徳先生（中部大学監事）、杉本和弘先生（中部大学学長顧問）に読んでいただき、貴重なご意見を賜った。それらはすべて訳に生かさせていただいた。ただ、もし誤訳などが残っていればすべて訳者二人の責任であることをお断りしておきたい。

一人でも多くの読者にベリーの思想に触れていただきたく、また訳については忌憚ないご意見をいただければ幸甚である。

＊凡例

一、訳文中の（　）は、原語の引用、もしくは原文中の記号（　），
　―　― である。

一、訳文中の［　］は、訳者による補足を示す。

I

大学の現状：
専門化と言葉の重要性

1）

大学における文学の苦境は、他のいかなる学問の苦境とも根本的に異なるものではなく、それは言語の苦境とも根本的に異なりません。すなわち、さまざまな学問分野が互いに言葉を交わすことをやめてしまったこと、学問分野があまりにも専門化しすぎてしまったこと、そしてこの過剰な専門化、分断が、それぞれの言語の専門化によって生み出され強化されてしまったのです。その結果、現代の大学は、何らかの統一原理に従う宇宙膨張とは異なり、雑な積み上げ原理に従う家具保管業者のように成長してきました。

The predicament of literature within the university is not fundamentally different from the predicament of any other discipline, which is not fundamentally different from the predicament of language. That is, the various disciplines have ceased to speak to each other; they have become too specialized, and this over-specialization, this separation, of the disciplines has been enabled and enforced by the specialization of their languages. As a result, the modern university has grown, not according to any unifying principle, like an expanding universe, but according to the principle of miscellaneous accretion, like a furniture storage business.

2）

ある程度の専門化は避けられないことであると思います。というのは、集中することで関心の幅は狭まるからです。私たちは、一度に一つのことしか集中できません。さらに、良い仕事をするには持続的な実践が必要なので、ある程度の専門化は望ましいと思います。もし私たちが、教えたり、書いたり、石を細工したり、農作業をする際に、最高の仕事をのぞむならば、その時は、長く優れた実践によって仕事の準備ができている人々、つまり腕ききの熟練労働者を手配しなければなりません。

I assume that there is a degree of specialization that is unavoidable because concentration involves a narrowing of attention; we can only do one thing at a time. I assume further that there is a degree of specialization that is desirable because good work depends upon sustained practice. If we want the best work to be done in teaching or writing or stone masonry or farming, then we must arrange for that work to be done by proven master workers, people who are prepared for the work by long and excellent practice.

3）

しかし、適切な専門化の程度があると仮定することは、同時に不適切な程度もあると仮定することです。私は、さまざまな種類の労働者が分断され、お互いに話すことをやめたときに、この不適切さが始まると考えています。この分断によって、労働者は、モノの**部品**だけの製造者になります。これが、産業［工業］組織がもたらす不適切さの正体です。エリック・ギル（訳注）はそのことについて次のように書いています。「労働者が作ったものに対して関心を持たなくなったとき、あるいは、労働者が作ったものに対してもはや何の責任も持たず、したがって、自分が作っているものが何であるかという知識を失ったとき、ものづくりの技術は、単なる器用さに退化し、つまり作業の技能に堕落してしまいます。工場労働者は自分が**やっている**ことしか知りません。何が作られているかは、彼の関心事ではありません」。現在の大学が抱える問題の一部（または問題の原因の一部）は、大学で作られるものに対する関心の喪失であり、その背後には、作られるものが何であるかについての合意の喪失があると私は考えています。

訳注　エリック・ギル（1882-1940）は、英国の社会哲学者、芸術家、活字書体デザイナー、作家。工業生産より手工業を重んじ、商業文明に対して人間性の回復を主張した。主な著作に『労働と余暇』（1935）、『キリスト教と機械時代』（1940）などがある。

But to assume that there is a degree of specialization that is proper is at the same time to assume that there is a degree that is improper. The impropriety begins, I think, when the various kinds of workers come to be divided and cease to speak to one another. In this division they become makers of **parts** of things. This is the impropriety of industrial organization, of which Eric Gill wrote, "Skill in making ... degenerates into mere dexterity, i.e. skill in doing, when the workman ... ceases to be concerned for the thing made or ... has no longer any responsibility for the thing made and has therefore lost the knowledge of what it is that he is making...The factory hand can only know what he is **doing**. What is being made is no concern of his." [NOTES 1] Part of the problem in universities now (or part of the cause of the problem) is this loss of concern for the thing made and, back of that, I think, the loss of agreement on what the things is that is being made.

原注1. Eric Gill, **A Holy Tradition of Working**, ed. Brian Keeble (Ipswich: Golgonooza Press, 1983), p. 61.

4）

大学で造り出されるものは、人間性です。大学の現在の影響力を考えれば、このことは当然なことです。しかし、大学、少なくとも公的支援を受ける大学が作り、あるいは養成の促進を**義務づけられている**ものは、この語の完全な意味での人間です。その人間は、単なる訓練された労働者や知識のある市民ではなく、人類文化の継承に責任をもつ社会の構成員です。大学の本来の仕事が人々に私的な野心を成し遂げるように教育するだけならば、どのように、私たちは公的な支援を正当化できるのでしょうか？もしも、公的な責任を果たすための市民を育てるだけなら、私たちは芸術や科学を教えることをどのように正当化できるのでしょうか？ ここでの共通の基準は、職業準備かまたは良い市民になる準備よりも大きいものでなければなりません。大学というものの根底にあるのは、あらゆる学問分野を一つにまとめ統合するということであり、良い仕事と良い市民性は、良い（つまり完全に成長した）人間を作るための必然的な副産物です。これこそが**大学**という名称の定義そのものだと私は理解しています。

The thing being made in a university is humanity. Given the current influence of universities, this is merely inevitable. But what universities, at least the public-supported ones, are **mandated** to make or to help to make is human beings in the fullest sense of those words — not just trained workers or knowledgeable citizens but responsible heirs and members of human culture. If the proper work of the university is only to equip people to fulfill private ambitions, then how do we justify public support? If it is only to prepare citizens to fulfill public responsibilities, then how do we justify the teaching of arts and sciences? The common denominator has to be larger than either career preparation or preparation for citizenship. Underlying the idea of a university — the bringing together, the combining into one, of all the disciplines — is the idea that good work and good citizenship are the inevitable by-products of the making of a good — that is, a fully developed — human being. This, as I understand it, is the definition of the name **university**.

5）

造られたものに関心をもち、さらにはそもそも何が造られているのかを把握するためには、大学全体が、学生全員や卒業生全員と同じ言葉を話さなければなりません。言い換えれば、そこでは共通の言葉が必要です。共通の言葉がなければ、大学は造られたものへの関心を失うだけでなく、大学自身の統一性をも失うことになります。さらに、ある大学の学部があまりにも専門化して、学部同士や他の学部の学生や卒業生と話せなくなってしまったら、その大学は居場所を失ってしまいます。そうなると、もはや大学は自分がどこにいるかわからなくなり、自分の場所に対する責任も、また自らの無責任の影響も理解できなくなります。これが、「学問の自由」の実際的な意味であることがあまりに多いのです。つまり、教師は、造られたものに関心を持つことなく、自由に教え、学び、ふるまい、考えているのです。

In order to be concerned for the thing made, in order even to know what it is making, the university as a whole must speak the same language as all of its students and all of its graduates. There must, in other words, be a common tongue. Without a common tongue, a university not only loses concern for the thing made; it loses its own unity. Furthermore, when the departments of a university become so specialized that they can speak neither to each other nor to the students and graduates of other departments, then that university is displaced. As an institution, it no longer knows where it is, and therefore it cannot know either its responsibilities to its place or the effects of its irresponsibility. This too often is the practical meaning of “academic freedom”: The teacher feels free to teach and learn, make and think, without concern for the thing made.

6）

たとえば、「土地供与大学」[訳注：農学、工学などの実学系の大学で、州政府より土地を供与されて設立された大学]では、農業研究者がより生産性の高い乳牛の開発に力を注ぐことが、次のような事実を全く考慮せずに容認されています。つまり、この開発は必ず何千もの酪農場と酪農家の破産を招くことをです。また、事実はすでにそうなっており、今後も必ずそうなることは避けられません。研究者は、単に「生産単位」とその生産量の比率に基づいて、そのような研究を正当化することが自由にできると思っています。そして、このような研究が続けられるのは、大学のほとんどすべての人、牛の乳を搾るほとんどすべての人、牛乳を飲むほとんどすべての人にとって、不可解で、おそらく理解できない言語でその研究が報告されているからと思われます。現代の大学が、そのような理系研究者に、例えば哲学、歴史、文学の文系同僚の前で自分の研究を弁護する場を提供する可能性は、今のところありません。また、哲学、歴史、文学系の学部・学科が、農業研究の倫理に関心を持ち、あるいは持とうとする同僚を数多く輩出する可能性もありません。

For example, it is still perfectly acceptable in land-grant universities for agricultural researchers to apply themselves to the development of more productive dairy cows without considering at all the fact that this development necessarily involves the failure of many thousands of dairies and dairy farmers — that it has already done so and will inevitably continue to do so. The researcher feels at liberty to justify such work merely on the basis of the ratio between the "production unit" and the volume of production. And such work is permitted to continue, I suspect, because it is reported in language that is unreadable and probably unintelligible to nearly everybody in the university, to nearly everybody who milks cows, and to nearly everybody who drinks milk. That a modern university might provide a forum in which such researchers might be required to defend their work before colleagues in, say, philosophy or history or literature is, at present, not likely, nor is it likely, at present, that the departments of philosophy, history, or literature could produce many colleagues able or willing to be interested in the ethics of agricultural research.

II

言葉の本質と大学の制限

7）

言葉はこの問題の核心にあります。何かを教えることは「だれかの前で信じるところを吐露する」ということです。それは、周囲の人や影響下にあるすべての人の前で言説することだと私は思います。しかし、その人の隣人や顧客の前で、ほとんどの人が理解できない言葉で述べるのでは、まったく「言説する」ことになっていません。特殊な専門語（professional language）とは、単に語義矛盾であるのみならず、ごまかしであり隠れ場所であり、まさに隠された罠です。専門職、言説（profession）および教授職（professorship）という概念の根底には、通常の言葉で誰にでもわかりやすく話さねばならないという必須事項があるのです。

Language is at the heart of the problem. To profess, after all, is "to confess before" — to confess, I assume, before all who live within the neighborhood or under the influence of the confessor. But to confess before one's neighbors and clients in a language that few of them can understand is not to confess at all. The specialized professional language is thus not merely a contradiction in terms; it is a cheat and a hiding place; it may, indeed, be an ambush. At the very root of the idea of profession and professorship is the imperative to speak plainly in the common tongue.

8）

したがって、その通常の言葉なるものが大学のある学科の排他的特殊物になるようなことがあればそれは悲劇です。それは、大学やその社会的立場にとっての悲劇であるのみならず、通常の言葉そのものにとっても悲劇です。それは、大学に関する限り、通常の言葉が通常の言葉では**なくなる**ことを意味します。それは、言葉たちの混乱状態の中の一つの言葉に過ぎなくなります。私たちの言葉や著作物は、世の中で起こっているものとは見なされず、大学の学科の中だけ、それらの言葉や書作物の中だけで起こっているものと見られるようになります。著作物は、通常の言葉を使うすべての読者の出会いの場ではなくなり、著作物についての耳障りなおしゃべりの場に過ぎなくなります。教師や学生たちは、素晴らしい歌や物語を読んで、そこ**から**何かを学ぶのではなく、その歌や物語に**ついて**学ぶためだけに読むことになります。アリの行列のあとを追うように**文章**をたどることはしても、そこに人生に影響を与える歌や物語の力というものを見出すことはありません。なぜなら、おそらくそれはほとんど感じとられないからです。

That the common tongue should become the exclusive specialty of a department in a university is therefore a tragedy, and not just for the university and its worldly place; it is a tragedy for the common tongue. It means that the common tongue, so far as the university is concerned, **ceases** to be the common tongue; it becomes merely one tongue within a confusion of tongues. Our language and literature cease to be seen as occurring in the world, and begin to be seen as occurring within their university department and within themselves. Literature ceases to be the meeting ground of all readers of the common tongue and becomes only the occasion of a deafening clatter **about** literature. Teachers and students read the great songs and stories to learn **about** them, not learn **from** them. The **texts** are tracked as by the passing of an army of ants, but the power of songs and stories to affect life is still little acknowledged, apparently because it is little felt.

9）

もちろん、このような専門家的アプローチは、部分的には正当化されるものです。話すことと書くことにおいて、言葉はそれ自体の中で生起するものです。言葉はそれ自体の中でこだまし、洞窟の中でこだまする声のように果てしなく反響し、そのこだまに応答し、その応答がまたこだまします。言葉というものはそうでなければなりません。つまり、言葉の本質は、ある程度、響き合うことにあるからです。（訳注）

訳注　プラトン『国家』第7巻にある「洞窟の比喩」参照。洞窟内にいて実体を伴わない「影」を「実体」と信じている人々は、発せられた偽りの言葉が洞窟内でこだまのように反響する中、確信を深めてしまう。

The specialist approach, of course, is partly justifiable; in both speech and literature, language does occur within itself. It echoes within itself, reverberating endlessly like a voice echoing within a cave, and speaking in answer to its echo, and the answer again echoing. It must do this; its nature, in part, is to do this.

10）

しかし、言葉の本質はまた、外部の世界に向かって、世の中の対象物を的確にヒットして残響を止めること、それらに一種の静止と静寂をもたらすことにもあります。言葉や言葉に関する研究の専門職化(professionalization)をすれば、洞窟のような反響は避けられません。人は内部の喧騒の中で休まることなくもがきつづけるのです。

But its nature also is to turn outward to the world, to strike its worldly objects cleanly and cease to echo — to achieve a kind of rest and silence in them. The professionalization of language and of language study makes the cave inescapable; one strives without rest in the interior clamor.

11）

語がその対象物に戻り、それらに触れ、そして語が止まった後の静けさは、耳を塞いだ状態の静けさではありません。それは、秋の最初の厳しい凍結の後、何週間も続いていたコオロギの鳴き声が突然止まった時、そして、幸いにも繰り返されるアクシデントで、すべての機械の音が一瞬止まった時に起こるような、世界の静けさです。それは準備して待たなければならない静けさであり、それはその人自身の静けさを必要とします。

The silence in which words return to their objects, touch them, and come to rest is not the silence of the plugged ear. It is the world's silence, such as occurs after the first hard freeze of autumn, when the weeks-long singing the crickets is suddenly stopped, and when, by a blessedly recurring accident, all machine noises have stopped for the moment, too. It is a silence that must be prepared for and waited for; it requires a silence of one's own.

12）

言葉それ自体の中におきる残響は、最終的には単なるノイズに過ぎません。それは、シンクタンクやその他の空虚な場所において、集められたデータが互いに無目的に軋み合って出されるノイズと似たり寄ったりのものです。データは、語と同様に、事物そのものではなく、事物の言葉による表象や記号であって、最終的には、それらが表すところの事物に帰着させて検証すべきものです。事物への回帰は専門家の仕事ではなく、普通の人間が行う行為ですが、適切に謙虚であって心静かな人だけがそれを行うことができます。その営為は私たちを、大きく伸ばしつつ形作り、解き放つとともに抑制するものなのです。

The reverberations of language within itself are, finally, mere noise, no better or worse than the noise of accumulated facts that grate aimlessly against each other in think tanks and other hollow places. Facts, like words, are not things but verbal tokens or signs of things that finally must be carried back to the things they stand for to be verified. This carrying back is not specialist work but an act generally human, though only properly humbled and quieted humans can do it. It is an act that at once enlarges and shapes, frees and limits us.

13）

例えば木の場合、**木**という語が、個人的かつ文化的な記憶を呼び起こすことが必要です。木が何であるかを完全に理解するためには、私たちがこれまで経験した多くのこと、そして木々について聞いたり読んだりしてきた多くのことを思い出す必要があります。私たちは、木々を単なることばとして考えたり、木々についての私たちの記憶を「文化史」として扱ったりすることで、それらの記憶を解体してしまいます。木を木と呼ぶとき、私たちはことばや事実の中で孤立しているのではなく、木そのものと一緒にいるのであり、これまで木々が存在し意味してきたことすべてを私たちに呼びかける先祖の声に囲まれています。これは、単にこの世界に生きる人間の条件であり、芸術や科学ができることは、それに慣れること以外にはありません。しかし、もちろん、専門的に「信じるところを告げる（professional）」芸術や科学だけが、それをどうにかしようと提案したり、望んだりするのです。

It is necessary, for example, that the word **tree** evoke memories that are both personal and cultural. In order to understand fully what a tree is, we must remember much of our experience with trees and much that we have heard and read about them. We destroy those memories by reducing trees to facts, by thinking of **trees** as a mere word, or by treating our memory of trees as "cultural history". When we call a tree a tree, we are not isolated among words and facts but are at once in the company of the tree itself and surrounded by ancestral voices calling out to us all that trees have been and meant. This is simply the condition of being human in this world, and there is nothing that art and science can do about it, except get used to it. But, of course, only specialized "professional" arts and sciences would propose or wish to do something about it.

14）

このように、語や事象が世界の中のそれぞれの対象物に立ち戻る必要があるということは、それが大学に課せられた境界の一つであり、どこであっても書物による学習の境界の一つを表します。そして、その境界の中では、謙虚さ、節度、厳格な規律、そして高い基準が必要となります。

This necessity for words and facts to return to their objects in the world describes one of the boundaries of a university, one of the boundaries of book learning anywhere, and it describes the need for humility, restraint, exacting discipline, and high standards within that boundary.

III
大学の崩壊と「生命の木」

15）

何かを作るという努力は、どんなものでも必ず狭くなるので、同時にその作ったものについての判断や批判の努力もできるだけ広範に行わなければなりません。つまり、作られたものはすべて、次のような問いを受けなければならないのです。それは、人間の作ったものとして、また、作られたものや創造されたものの世界に加わるものとして、そのものの質は確かなものでしょうか？　さらに、それは、人間や自然界にどれだけ必要なものでしょうか？

Beside every effort of making, which is necessarily narrow, there must be an effort of judgment, of criticism, which must be as broad as possible. That is, every made thing must be submitted to these questions: What is the quality of this thing as a human artifact, as an addition to the world of made and of created things? How suitable is it to the needs of human and natural neighborhoods?

16）

もちろん、遅かれ早かれ、特別な疑問も提出されるでしょう。この詩、この農場、この病院は、それ自体、どれほど優れたものなのでしょうか？それが人間的な価値を持つためには、明らかにうまく作られていなければならないし、専門的な技術基準を満たしていなければならず、また、それ自体**優れたもの**であるべきです。しかし、そのような質に関する問いは、より一般的な問いのルールに基づいて問うのでなければ、興味深いものではなく、長い目で見れば、おそらく問うことすらできないでしょう。もし私たちが、より大きな問いから切り離して判断する傾向があるならば、また、専門家として判断するのであれば、優れた偽物の作り手は、優れた芸術家と同様に、私たちの尊敬を受ける正当な権利をもつことになります。

It must, of course, sooner or later be submitted as well to the special question: How good is this poem or this farm or this hospital as such? For it to have a human value, it obviously must be well made; it must meet the specialized, technical criteria; it must be **good** as such. But the question of its quality as such is not interesting — in the long run it is probably not even askable — unless we ask it under the rule of the more general questions. If we are disposed to judge apart from the larger questions, if we judge, as well as make, as specialists, then a good forger has as valid a claim to our respect as a good artist.

17)

この二つの問題、「どう作るか」と「どう判断するか」は、教育の問題です。しかし、教育は、その責任の二重性をますます無視する傾向にあります。教育は、「どう作るか」という問題だけに集中してきました。そして、判断の問題を、作られたもの自体の関係に事実上狭めてきたのです。しかし、今、教育によって作られる人間は、完全に発達した人間ではなく、単なる専門家、キャリア主義者(出世第一主義者)、卒業生に過ぎません。産業(工業)教育では、**最終的に**作られるものは作る側にとっては何の関心もありません。

These two problems, how to make and how to judge, are the business of education. But education has tended increasingly to ignore the doubleness of its obligation. It has concerned itself more and more exclusively with the problem of how to make, narrowing the issue of judgment virtually to the terms of the made thing itself. But the thing made by education now is not a fully developed human being; it is a specialist, a careerist, a graduate. In industrial education, the thing **finally** made is of no concern to the makers.

18)

これは、専門的な「分野」が複雑になりすぎて、判断に必要な幅の広い基礎的な科目を学ぶ時間がカリキュラムに残されていないことが原因の場合もあります。また、広く情報を得て判断することと、学生が目指している専門的なキャリアとの間に、潜在的に様々な問題を引き起こすような矛盾があると感じる場合もあります。例えば、広告技術を教える教師は、嘘やそそのかしの技術を学んでいることを学生に理解させる余裕はありません。いずれの場合も、この狭められたカリキュラムは、若い学生は何も知らないうちから自分が何を学ぶべきかを知っているというありえない仮定によって、正当化されているのです。

In some instances this is because the specialized "fields" have grown so complicated within themselves that the curriculum leaves no time for the broad and basic studies that would inform judgment. In other instances, one feels that there is a potentially embarrassing conflict between judgment broadly informed and the specialized career for which the student is being prepared; teachers of advertising techniques, for example, could ill afford for their students to realize that they are learning the arts of lying and seduction. In all instances, this narrowing is justified by the improbable assumption that young students, before they know anything else, know what they need to learn.

19)

大学の崩壊が専門家重視のイデオロギーから始まるとすれば、それは顧客を満足させようとする商業的な圧力によって強化されることになります。学生が自分の教育を決定する自由な主体となっている今、学部・学科の管理者や教員は、いかにして入学者数を維持するかという問題に必ず頭を悩まされるはずです。学生定員を満たすために明らかに何かを行う必要があります。さもないと、学生はより魅力的なコースまたは提案されたキャリアに直接役立つコースに流れることになります。このような状況下では、必要な条件が緩和され、基準が引き下げられ、成績が引き上げられ、指導が何らかのキャリアの機会を想定した要件に狭められることは避けられません。

If the disintegration of the university begins in its specialist ideology, it is enforced by a commercial compulsion to satisfy the customer. Since the student is now so much a free agent in determining his or her education, the department administrators and the faculty members must necessarily be preoccupied with the problem of how to keep enrollments up. Something obviously must be done to keep the classes filled; otherwise, the students will wander off to more attractive courses or to courses more directly useful to their proposed careers. Under such circumstances it is inevitable that requirements will be lightened, standards lowered, grades inflated, and instruction narrowed to the supposed requirements of some supposed career opportunity.

20)

ジョンソン博士は、従兄弟のコーネリウス・フォードから次のような助言を受けたとスレイル夫人に語っています(訳注1)。「彼は、万物の原理を研究し、その結果、人生について一般的な知識が得られるかもしれないと助言してくれた。また彼は、万事に先立つ主要なことを学べと言った、つまり……木の幹だけを強く掴めば、すべての枝を揺らすことになるだろう、と」。このアドバイスの正しさには議論の余地がなく、この比喩もまったく適切なものです。つまり、幹から出発し「枝分かれ」することは可能です。幹から一つの枝を伸ばすこともできるし、いくつもの枝を伸ばすこともできます。しかし、枝から出発して幹を伸ばすことは可能かもしれませんが、その可能性は高くもなく、有望でもありません。いずれにしても、現代の大学は、ますます無造作に空中を舞っている切り落とされた枝の緩い集合体に似てきています。「現代の知識は細分化されている」とH. J. マッシンガムは1943年に書き、続けて「しかし、文化の本質は全体性への導入であり、そのため知識のすべての部門は、一本の木の枝とみなされる、そしてその生命の木の根は地中に深くはいりこみ、その樹冠は天上にあると」と述べています(訳注2)。

訳注1　サミュエル・ジョンソン(1709-84)は、イングランドの詩人、批評家、随筆家。『英語辞典』(1755)の編集で知られる。文壇の大御所であると同時に豊かな人間的感情の持主として、広く敬愛を集めた。　文中に出てくる、従兄弟のコーネリウス・フォードは、知的に洗練された学識ある人物で、サミュエルはこの従兄弟から多大な影響を受けた。　また、スレイル夫人は、18世紀後半の英国における教養ある上流夫人の集まり「ブルーストッキング(青鞜)」の中心人物の一人で、サミュエルもこの集まりに参加していたことから親しい関係にあった。

訳注2　H. J. マッシンガム(1888-1952)は、英国の作家、詩人。田園生活と農業について多くの著作を残した。

Dr. Johnson told Mrs. Thrale that his cousin, Cornelius Ford, "advised him to study the Principles of everything, that a general Acquaintance with Life might be the Consequence of his Enquiries — Learn said he the leading Precognita of all things ... grasp the Trunk hard only, and you will shake all the Branches." (2) The soundness of this advice seems indisputable, and the metaphor entirely apt. From the trunk it is possible to "branch out." One can begin with a trunk and develop a single branch or any number of branches; although it may be possible to begin with a branch and develop a trunk, that is neither so probable nor so promising. The modern university, at any rate, more and more resembles a loose collection of lopped branches waving about randomly in the air. "Modern knowledge is departmentalized," H. J. Massingham wrote in 1943, "while the essence of culture is initiation into wholeness, so that all the divisions of knowledge are considered as the branches of one tree, the Tree of Life whose roots went deep into earth and whose top was in heaven." (3)

原注2.　W. Jackson Bate, **Samuel Johnson** (New York: Harcourt Brace Jovanovich, 1977), p. 51.

原注3.　H. J. Massingham, **The Tree of Life** (London: Chapman & Hall, 1943).

21)

この木は、何百年にもわたって、私たちが知識の形を説明しようとするときに、まったく自然に頭に浮かんでくるものです。西洋の伝統では、この木は少なくとも「創世記」と同じくらいの古い歴史があり、私たちが知っているすべてのものに対して、有機的、統一的、包括的、連帯的、さらに道徳的な形を与えてくれます。最初、この木は、生命の木と善悪の知識の木という二本の木でした。その後、私たちの理解では、この二本の木は一本になったように見えたり、またそれぞれがもう一方の木を表わしているようにも見えます。人間の堕落後の世界では、この二つの木をどうやって分けることができるのでしょうか？人生を知ることは、善と悪を知ることであり、若者の人生への備えは、善と悪の違いを知るための準備です。知識を木として表現するならば、分割されたものはまだつながっていることがわかります。私たちは、分割を観察し、つながりを無視することは、木を破壊することだと知っています。近代教育の歴史は、この木のイメージの喪失の歴史かもしれないし、分割の上に成り立つ産業（工業）機械のあり方、分割を離れては意味をなさない産業（工業）経済学（「成果・論文を出すかそれとも消え去るか」（訳注））、によって取って代わられた歴史なのかもしれません。

訳注　原文は“publish or perish”。一般に医・理系の学界では、「研究成果を論文として発表・出版し続けなければ、生き残れない」という意味でこの言葉が使われている。

This Tree, for many hundreds of years, seems to have come almost naturally to mind when we have sought to describe the form of knowledge. In Western tradition, it is at least as old as Genesis, and the form it gives us for all that we know is organic, unified, comprehensive, connective — and moral. The tree, at the beginning, was two trees: the tree of life and the tree of knowledge of good and evil. Later, in our understanding of them, the two trees seem to have become one, or each seems to stand for the other — for in the world after the Fall, how can the two be separated? To know life is to know good and evil; to prepare young people for life is to prepare them to know the difference between good and evil. If we represent knowledge as a tree, we know that things that are divided are yet connected. We know that to observe the divisions and ignore the connections is to destroy the tree. The history of modern education may be the history of the loss of this image, and of its replacement by the pattern of the industrial machine, which subsists upon division — and by industrial economics ("publish or perish"), which is meaningless apart from division.

IV
「キャリア準備」教育の本質と「木の幹」教育

22)

それでもやはり、幅広い知識を持つ人間の判断が必要であることに変わりはなく、そのためには幅広い基礎的な教育が必要であることは言うまでもありません。このような私的**かつ**公的な必要性に対して、「キャリア準備」教育は単に私的な目的のためなので、それは公的資金の不適切な使用です。また、「キャリア準備」は雇用者の監督下での見習い期間中に最も効率よく、適切に習得されるものなので、学生の時間の浪費です。例えば、学校において本来学ぶべきことは、上手に話し、書く方法であって、「講演者」、「アナウンサー」、「クリエイティブライター」、「テクニカルライター」、ジャーナリストや、「ビジネス英語」の実践者にどのようにしてなるかということではありません。もし、うまく話したり書いたりできれば、必要に応じて、その人はスピーチができ、記事か小説かビジネスレターが書けるはずです。うまく話したり、書いたりできないのであれば、その人には商売のコツなどはまったく役に立ちません。

The need for broadly informed human judgment nevertheless remains, and this need requires inescapably an education that is broad and basic. In the face of this need, which is **both** private and public, "career preparation" is an improper use of public money, since "career preparation" serves merely private ends; it is also a waste of the student's time, since "career preparation" is best and most properly acquired in apprenticeships under the supervision of employers. The proper subject for a school, for example, is how to speak and write well, not how to be a "public speaker" or a "broadcaster" or a "creative writer" or a "technical writer" or a journalist or a practitioner of "business English." If one can speak and write well, then, given the need, one can make a speech or write an article or a story or a business letter. If one cannot speak or write well, then the tricks of a trade will be no help.

23)

大学を統合すべき仕事、またそれを通じて大学の統合が可能になる仕事とは、学生に何を学ばせるか、つまり、どのような学問がその人の教育の「木の幹」を構成するかを決定することです。学問の専門化を実質的に支えてきた（そして学問の専門家に多くの報酬を与えてきた）「キャリア準備」教育は、この問題への関心を破壊してしまったようです。しかし、この問題は存在するし、それに答えない（あるいは問うこともしない）ことは、教師、学生、そして一般市民に重大な不利益を課すことになります。基礎教育を広く渉猟しなかったことに対して学生や卒業生に課せられる不利益は、十分に明白だと思います。また、例えば専門家として認定されている講演者や作家の中には、解りやすく話したり書いたりできない人、自分の話し方や書き方が悪いことに気づいていない人、正直に話したり書いたりしているかどうかを気にしない人がいることを考えれば、公共への不利益は明らかです。

The work that should, and that can, unify a university is that of deciding what a student should be required to learn — what studies, that is, constitute the trunk of the tree of a person's education. "Career preparation," which has given so much practical support to academic specialization (and so many rewards to academic specialists) seems to have destroyed interest in this question. But the question exists and the failure to answer it (or even to ask it) imposes severe penalties on teachers, students, and the public alike. The penalties imposed on students and graduates by their failure to get a broad, basic education are, I think, obvious enough. The public penalties are also obvious if we consider, for instance, the number of certified expert speakers and writers who do not speak or write well, who do not know that they speak or write poorly, and who apparently do not care whether or not they speak or write honestly.

24)

この失敗が教師に課す不利益は、これまでこの不利益が報酬によって隠されてきたために、あまりはっきりしていません。教師にとっての不利益は、学生や一般市民にとっての不利益と同じですが、それに加えてもう一つあります。つまり、学生が何を学ぶべきかを決められないと、その教師は責任ある大人として機能することができないばかりか、またおそらく責任ある大人になることもできません。

The penalties that this failure imposes on teachers are not so obvious, mainly, I suppose, because so far the penalties have been obscured by rewards. The penalties for teachers are the same as those for students and the public, plus one more: The failure to decide what students should be required to learn keeps the teacher from functioning as, and perhaps from becoming, a responsible adult.

25)

若者に教えるのは年長（年配）の人以外にはいないので、年長の人がそれをやらなければなりません。年長の人がそれをするにあたって十分な知識を持っていないこと、また十分な才覚や経験、能力を持っていないことは重要ではありません。他にそれをする人がいない以上、彼らはそれをしなければならないのです。これはまさに人生の本質的な試練であり、人によってはこれを「本質的な悲劇」とも言います。つまり、この教育は、利用可能な知識だけに基づいて進める必要があります。また、その知識が十分かどうか、真実かどうかという問題は遅くまで先延ばしにする必要があります。

There is no one to teach young people but older people, and so the older people must do it. That they do not know enough to do it, that they have never been smart enough or experienced enough or good enough to do it, does not matter. They must do it because there is no one else to do it. This is simply the elemental trial — some would say the elemental tragedy — of human life: the necessity to proceed on the basis merely of the knowledge that is available, the necessity to postpone until too late the question of the sufficiency and the truth of that knowledge.

26)

したがって、人間の教育には、試行錯誤という避けられない要素があります。教えられることの中には間違っていることもあります、なぜなら、誤りを犯す可能性のある人間が教師だからです。しかし、教育、その絶え間ない努力と鍛錬の理由は、若者の試行錯誤への依存を可能な限り減らすことにあるのは確かです。なぜなら試行錯誤への依存は、減らすことが**できる**からです。人は、すべてのことを、あるいは基本的なことを試行錯誤によって学ばなくてもよいからです。子供は、火の中に落ちることで熱の危険性を学ぶ必要はありません。学生は、非識字者であることによって非識字者の不利益を学んだり、劣悪な「体験学習」によって良い教育の価値を学ぶ必要はありません。

There is, then, an inescapable component of trial and error in human education; some things that are taught will be wrong because fallible humans are the teachers. But the reason for education, its constant effort and discipline, is surely to reduce the young person's dependence on trial and error as far as possible. For it **can** be reduced. One should not have to learn everything, or the basic things, by trial and error. A child should not have to learn the danger of heat by falling into the fire. A student should not have to learn the penalties of illiteracy by being illiterate or the value of a good education by the "object lesson" of a poor one.

27)

教師は「キャリア準備」教育をしているのではなく、「若者に人生への準備をさせている」のです。この見解は教育理論から生まれたものではなく、単なる事実です。若者が人生の準備をするために、教師は知識を提供し、無知を啓発しなければなりません。しかし無知は、教育が解決しようとする苦悩であるだけではなく、それはまた、教育が行われるための条件であり、苦境でもあるのです。なぜなら、教師は学生が準備しようとしている人生や生活を知り得ないからです。

Teachers, moreover, are not providing "career preparation" so much as they are "preparing young people for life." This statement is not the result of educational doctrine; it is simply the fact of the matter. To prepare young people for life, teachers must dispense knowledge and enlighten ignorance, just as supposed. But ignorance is not only the affliction that teaching seeks to cure; it is also the condition, the predicament, in which teaching is done, for teachers do not know the life or the lives for which their students are being prepared.

28)

このような状況では、「キャリア準備」教育という主張は嘘になります。なぜなら、学生は準備した通りのキャリアを**持てない**かもしれないからです。つまり、「求人倍率」が高くなりすぎたり、職業に必要な条件が変わったり、学生が変わったり、世の中が変わるかもしれません。教師には、彼らの両方（教師と学生）にとって必然的に未知な人生に向けて学生に準備させるにあたり、学生が「木の幹を掴む」ことを手伝う以外に選択の余地はありません。

This condition gives the lie to the claims for “career preparation,” since students may not **have** the careers for which they have been prepared: The “job market” may be overfilled; the requirements for this or that career may change; the student may change, or the world may. The teacher, preparing the student for a life necessarily unknown to them both, has no excusable choice but to help the student to “grasp the Trunk.”

29)

しかし、「キャリア準備」を求める議論は今も行われており、その意欲はますます高まっています。例えば、1983年8月23日、『アソシエイテッド・プレス（Associated Press）』は、「テキサス州教育委員会の長が、小学6年生に職業訓練の職業『選択』を義務づけることを望んでいる」と報じています。このように、12歳の子どもたちが、自分の望む人生を「自由に選ぶ」ことができるとされているのです。この記事によれば、「キャリア・トラック［職業コース］」を変更することも自由ですが、その場合には卒業が遅れるというペナルティがあるとのことです。

Yet the arguments for "career preparation" continue to be made and to grow in ambition. On August 23, 1983, for example, the Associated Press announced that "the head of the Texas school board wants to require sixth-graders to choose career 'tracks' that will point them toward jobs." (4) Thus, twelve-year-old children would be "free to choose" the kind of life they wish to live. They would even be free to change "career tracks," though, according to the article, such a change would involve the penalty of a delayed graduation.

原注4. "Texas School Board Chief Wants Sixth-Graders to Pick Job 'Tracks,'" **Courier-Journal** (Louisville, Ky.) 13 Aug. 1983.

30)

しかし、これらは準備ができていない、もしくは準備しつつある子どもたちに与えられた自由な「選択」です。この考え方は実際には、大人の選択を子供に押し付けるものであり、この「選択」は、最も悪質な経済的決定論を覆い隠しています。「キャリア・トラック［職業コース］」教育という考えは、教育、授業、子供時代、未来など、これに関わるすべてのものを委縮させてしまうものです。そして、そのようなことは、それが既に大学やカレッジの学部課程に組み込まれてしまっているのでない限り、［テキサスのように］それを小学6年生に適用しようなどとは思いもよらないことでしょう。

But these are free choices granted to children not prepared or ready to make them. The idea, in reality, is to impose adult choices on children, and these "choices" mask the most vicious sort of economic determinism. This idea of education as "career track" diminishes everything it touches: education, teaching, childhood, the future. And such a thing could not be contemplated for sixth-graders, obviously, if it had not already been instituted in the undergraduate programs of colleges and universities.

31)

まだ何も知らない勉強のコースやキャリアのコースを選択することを若者に要求したり、期待したり、あるいは許可したりすることは、主張されているような自由の付与では決してありません。それは、むしろ自由を著しく制限するものです。これは実際には、学生が学校を卒業し、適切にキャリアを選択する必要に迫られたときに、一つしか選択できないことを意味します。その時点で学生は、何年も前に無駄に与えられ、まさに無駄に与えられたことによって没収されてしまったところの「選択の自由」が無くて立ち尽くすのです。

To require or expect or even allow young people to choose courses of study and careers that they do not yet know anything about is not, as is claimed, a grant of freedom. It is a severe limitation upon freedom. It means, in practice, that when the student has finished school and is faced then, appropriately, with the need to choose a career, he or she is prepared to choose only one. At that point, the student stands in need of a freedom of choice uselessly granted years before and forfeited in that grant.

32)

若者に何を教えるかを決めるのは、大人たちの責任です。大人たちがこの責任を若者に転嫁するとき、それが無関心であろうと自由の付与であろうと、大人たちは一種の子供じみた行為に陥っているのです。その責任を引き受けなければ、教師自身の学識や人格が発揮されることはありません。そして、現代の産業［工業］化された教育システムにおいて、教師の学識と人格は、官僚的で方法論的な手続き、「雇用市場」の仕様、機械採点によるテストといったものに簡単に取って代わられるのです。

The responsibility to decide what to teach the young is an adult responsibility. When adults transfer this responsibility to the young, whether they do it by indifference or as a grant of freedom, they trap themselves in a kind of childishness. In that failure to accept responsibility, the teacher's own learning and character are disemployed, and, in the contemporary industrialized education system, they are easily replaced by bureaucratic and methodological procedures, "job market" specifications, and tests graded by machines.

33)

すべての若者が何を学ぶべきかというこの問題は、現在ほとんど議論されていません。その理由は、専門性がこれほどまでに求められ、しかも多様化している現在、このような質問に答えることは不可能ではないにしても、非常に困難であるという暗黙の了解があるからだと思われます。しかし、この問題は、他のどの問題とも同様に、理性と常識の範囲内にあると思います。そもそも、すべての学問が文字の知識と数字の知識の上に成り立つことは否定できません。数字よりも文字を重視する人もいれば、文字よりも数字を重視する人もいます。しかし、文字と数字の両方の知識を知らない人は、他のことを学ぶ準備ができていないということになります。そこから、歴史、文学、哲学、外国語は主に文字の知識に基づいて、それを進めていくものであり、生物学、化学、物理学は数字の知識に基づいて、それを進めていくものであると自信を持って言えます。このことから、おそらく適切な「コア・カリキュラム」の説明ができます。つまり、学生が進学の方向を選択し、その方向に進むための十分な準備ができるようなカリキュラムです。同様に明らかに必要なことは、そのカリキュラムから内容のないコースをすべて排除することです。つまり実習で学ぶことができ、また学ぶべき方法論や技術のコースをなくすことです。

This question of what all young people should be expected to learn is now little discussed. The reason, apparently, is the tacit belief that now, with the demands of specialization so numerous and varied, such a question would be extremely hard, if not impossible, to answer. And yet this question appears to be as much within the reach of reason and common sense as any other. It cannot be denied, to begin with, that all the disciplines rest upon the knowledge of letters and the knowledge of numbers. Some rest more on letters than numbers, some more on numbers than letters, but it is surely true to say that people without knowledge of both letters and numbers are not prepared to learn much else. From there, one can proceed confidently to say that history, literature, philosophy, and foreign languages rest principally on the knowledge of letters and carry it forward, and that biology, chemistry, and physics rest on the knowledge of numbers and carry it forward. This provides us with a description of a probably adequate "core curriculum" — one that would prepare a student well both to choose a direction of further study and to go in that direction. An equally obvious need, then, is to eliminate from the curriculum all courses without content— that is, all courses in methodologies and technologies that could, and should, be learned in apprenticeships.

V
「学校での失敗」と「大学への期待と基準」

34)

すでに述べた人間の生来の欠陥のほかにも、学生が自分で教育進路の選択をすることに期待し、要求することには、他の困難な問題も関わっています。これらの問題は、主に才能や能力の多様性に関係しています。つまり、ある種の仕事や研究には才能がない人もいるし、ある分野は苦手でも、別の分野では得意な人もいます。それなのに、なぜそのような人々が、自分自身を不出来な労働者や失敗者として見なければならないような状況に追い込まれてしまうのでしょうか？

Besides the innate human imperfections already mentioned, other painful problems are involved in expecting and requiring students to choose the course of their own education. These problems have to do mainly with the diversity of gifts and abilities: that is, some people are not talented in some kinds of work or study; some, moreover, who are poor in one discipline may be excellent in another. Why should such people be forced into situations in which they must see themselves as poor workers or as failures?

35)

この問題は快適なものではないし、また快適に答えられるものでも、そうすべきとも思っていません。失敗のリスクを伴う要求には痛みがあり、その要求によって生じるかもしれない失敗にも痛みが伴います。しかし、失敗は可能性であり、程度の差こそあれ、誰にとっても避けられないものです。したがって、学業から失敗の可能性を排除しようとする議論は、必然的に疑わしいものとなります。問題は、学生を失敗の可能性にさらすことや、学生の失敗を失敗と呼ぶことにはありません。間違いは、学校での失敗が必ずしも世間での失敗と同じではなく、また必ずしもそれが世間での失敗につながるものではないということを教師が理解できていないことにあります。その誤りは、学校と世間との間にある境界を認め、尊重することができないことにあります。その境界が認識され、尊重されない場合、学校や学校でのキャリア、卒業証書はすべて、偽りで支配的な威厳に包まれ、学校での失敗が、世間での失敗に**なってしまうのです**。教育に金銭的価値を与え、教育を消費者に十把ひとからげで売り込むことが簡単なのはこの理由によります。

The question is not a comfortable one, and I do not believe that it can or should be comfortably answered. There is pain in the requirement to risk failure and pain in the failure that may result from that requirement. But failure is a possibility; in varying degrees for all of us, it is inescapable. The argument for removing the possibility of failure from schoolwork is therefore necessarily specious. The wrong is not in subjecting students to the possibility of failure or in calling their failures failures; the wrong is in the teacher's inability to see that failure in school is not necessarily synonymous with and does not necessarily lead to failure in the world. The wrong is in the failure to see or respect the boundaries between the school and the world. When those are not understood and respected, then the school, the school career, the diploma are all surrounded by such a spurious and modish dignity that failure in school **is** failure in the world. It is for this reason that it is so easy to give education a money value and to sell it to consumers in job lots.

36)

頭脳明晰な人の中には、学校に馴染めず、学校の基準やテストでは正当に評価されていない人がいるのは事実です。そのような人が学校で失敗した場合、その失敗は「学校での失敗」と呼ばれるべきです。学校の価値とそのあるべき姿は、物事を正しい名前で呼ぼうとする意欲にかかっています。しかし、同じ理由で、学校での失敗はそれ以上のものではありません。学校での失敗は必ずしも愚かさを示したり引き起こしたりするものではなく、世間での失敗を示したり引き起こしたりするものでもありません。世間の判断が、学校の判断を覆すことはよくあることです。人間の能力を測るテストは、学校で行うもの以外にもあり、学校では行うことができないものもあります。私自身の生活の中で、高校には通っていないが、自分の「分野」に精通し、一般的な重要事項について、私が知っているほとんどの哲学者よりも優れた発言をしていた人を偶然に何人も知っています。これは「反知性」的な発言ではなく、私が事実だと思うことを述べたもので、学校の役割が限られているということだけを意味しているに過ぎません。他にも、学校は私たちに意外なことを教えてくれます。

It is a fact that some people with able minds do not fit well into schools and are not properly valued by schoolish standards and tests. If such people fail in a school, their failure should be so called; a school's worth and integrity depend upon its willingness to call things by their right names. But, by the same token, a failure in school is no more than that; it does not necessarily imply or cause failure in the world, any more than it implies or causes stupidity. It is not rare for the judgment of the world to overturn the judgment of schools. There are other tests for human abilities than those given in schools, and there are some that cannot be given in schools. My own life has happened to acquaint me with several people who did not attend high school but who have been more knowledgeable in their "field" and who have had better things to say about matters of general importance than most of the doctors of philosophy I have known. This is not an "anti-intellectual" statement; it is a statement of what I take to be fact, and it means only that the uses of schools are limited — another fact, which schools prepare us to learn by surprise.

37)

もう一つ考えるべき重要なことは、大学側の期待や基準が低いと、高校や小学校側の期待と基準も低くなるということです。もしも、大学が大学の期待と基準を引き上げれば、高校や小学校もその期待と基準を必ず引き上げるでしょうし、そうせざるを得ないのです。一方で、大学は、学生が大学の授業を受ける準備ができていないからといって高校レベルの授業を実施すると、それは高校から高校がやるべきことを取り除き、高校を楽にさせるだけであり、その過程で大学は自分の義務を果たせなくなります。いったん学校が学生に合わせて身を屈めてしまえば、あらゆるレベルでの判断基準は揺らぎ始めます。つまり、基準が下がると、大学が学生を測るのではなく大学が学生に測られるようになり、それにつれて学生が失敗する可能性は明らかに低くなります。しかし、同じ理由で、学生が学ぶことができる可能性も教師が教えることができる可能性も低くなります。

Another necessary consideration is that low expectations and standards in universities encourage the lowering of expectations and standards in the high schools and elementary schools. If the universities raise their expectations and standards, the high schools and elementary schools will raise theirs; they will have to. On the other hand, if the universities teach high school courses because the students are not prepared for university courses, then they simply relieve the high schools of their duty and in the process make themselves unable to do their own duty. Once the school stoops to meet the student, the standards of judgment begin to topple at all levels. As standards are lowered — as they cease to be the measure of the students and come to be measured by them — it becomes manifestly less possible for students to fail. But for the same reason it becomes less possible for them to learn and for teachers to teach.

38)

そこで問題は、何が教育の型を決めるのかということです。私たちは、高い期待や基準を満たすことができないと思われる学生の過去の学校教育や、私たちにとってまだはっきりしない未来の学生の必要性に応じて、大学教育を形成しなければならないのでしょうか？　それとも、「万事に先立つ主要なこと」の特質と求めに従って、つまり、学問が本質的に主題とすることに基づいて大学教育を形成するのでしょうか？　もし私たちが学生に合わせて教育を形成するならば、私たちは明らかに何の基準も維持することができないし、私たちは必ず最終的に学問の本質と学生を同時に失います。もしも学問の本質に合わせた教育をすれば、学問と学生の両方を必ず救うことができます。教育の避けられない目的は、人間にとって本質的な手段、つまり、思考と語と仕事と方法と基準と希望を保全し、継承することにあります。つまり、これらの手段なしに私たちは人間であることができません。これらのものを保存し、継承することが、学生の人生への準備となります。

The question, then, is what is to determine the pattern of education. Shall we shape a university education according to the previous schooling of the students, which we suppose has made them unfit to meet high expectations and standards, and to the supposed needs of students in some future still dark to us all? Or shall we shape it according to the nature and demands of the "leading Precognita of all things"— that is, according to the essential subjects of study? If we shape education to fit the students, then we clearly can maintain no standards; we will lose the subjects and eventually will lose the students as well. If we shape it to the subjects, then we will save both the subjects and the students. The inescapable purpose of education must be to preserve and pass on the essential human means — the thoughts and words and works and ways and standards and hopes without which we are not human. To preserve these things and to pass them on is to prepare students for life.

39)

このような仕事は、高い基準がなければできないことは言うまでもありません。学年と学齢が上がるにつれて、学習内容は必ず複雑さを増しますが、その基準は変わりません。小学校1年生は、つまり簡単な文章を読み書きしなければなりませんが、それでもキング・ジェームズ版聖書[訳注1]やシェイクスピア[訳注2]、サミュエル・ジョンソン、ヘンリー・ソロー[訳注3]、ウォルター・ホイットマン[訳注4]、エミリー・ディキンソン[訳注5]、マーク・トウェイン[訳注6]などにある言葉を使って読み書きをします。小学生も大学院生も同じアメリカの歴史を学ばなければならず、それを初歩的なものにするために改竄することは許されません。

訳注1　キング・ジェームズ版聖書は、イングランド王ジェームズ1世の命令で1611年に作られた英訳聖書で欽定訳聖書とも言われる。簡潔かつ格調高い文体から、英語、英文学に与えた影響は甚大とされる。

訳注2　シェークスピア（1564-1616）は、イングランドの詩人、劇作家。最も有名で優れた英文学作家の一人。『ハムレット』(1601頃)『マクベス』(1606頃)『ロミオとジュリエット』(1595頃）など。

訳注3　ヘンリー・ソロー（1817-1862）は、アメリカの随筆家。湖畔に建てた小屋でほぼ自給自足の生活をし『ウォールデン－森の生活』(1584)を著した。エコロジー思想の先駆として後世に大きな影響を及ぼした。

訳注4　ウォルター・ホイットマン（1819-1892）は、アメリカの詩人、随筆家、ジャーナリスト。主著『草の葉』(1855）は、伝統的な詩とは異なる自由な表現・内容の詩として名高い。

訳注5　エミリー・ディキンソン（1830-1886）は、アメリカの詩人。死後1800篇におよぶ優れた詩が発見された。現在ではアメリカ最高の詩人の一人と認められている。

訳注6　マーク・トウェイン（1835-1910）アメリカの作家。著書『トム・ソーヤーの冒険』(1876)『ハックルベリー・フィンの冒険』(1885)を生き生きとした口語で著しアメリカの国民文学を作り上げた。

That such work cannot be done without high standards ought not to have to be said. There are necessarily increasing degrees of complexity in the studies as students rise through the grades and the years, and yet the standards remain the same. The first-graders, that is, must read and write in simple sentences, but they read and write, even so, in the language of the King James Bible, of Shakespeare and Johnson, of Thoreau, Whitman, Dickinson, and Twain. The grade-schooler and the graduate student must study the same American history, and there is no excuse for falsifying it in order to make it elementary.

40)

さらに、基準を維持するためには、それらを特殊化、専門化、細分化することはできません。共通の基準、つまりコミュニティ全体で共通に保持され、支持される基準のみが維持され得るのです。例えば、大学で英作文を英語学部・学科や新入生英語コースだけで担当するようになると、作文コースの作品の質は低下し、その水準が下がります。これは必ず、そして明白な理由で起こります。もし学生の作文が作文の授業では形式と質に応じて評価されるが、例えば歴史の授業では「内容」に応じてのみ評価され、他の授業では作文をまったく要求されないとなれば、学生へのメッセージは次のように明白なものとなります。つまり、作文の形式と質は作文クラスでのみ重要だが、実際にはほとんど重要ではないというメッセージです。作文の高い基準は、大学のあらゆる場所でその高い基準が維持されている場合にのみ維持されるのです。

Moreover, if standards are to be upheld, they cannot be specialized, professionalized, or departmented. Only common standards can be upheld – standards that are held and upheld in common by the whole community. When, in a university, for instance, English composition is made the responsibility exclusively of the English department, or of the subdepartment of freshman English, then the quality of the work in composition courses declines and the standards decline. This happens necessarily and for an obvious reason: If students' writing is graded according to form and quality in composition class but according only to "content" in, say, history class and if in other classes students are not required to write at all, then the message to the students is clear: namely, that the form and quality of their writing matters only in composition class, which is to say that it matters very little indeed. High standards of composition can be upheld only if they are upheld everywhere in the university.

41)

基準は、共通して保持され、維持されなければならないだけでなく、公正に適用されなければなりません。つまり、個人や集団に関して条件があってはなりません。いかなる理由であれ、いかなる人に対しても差別があってはなりません。個々の実施者の質が問題であり、実施者の属性が問題ではありません。目的は、優れた仕事を認識し、報奨し、促進することです。歴史的、経済的、教育的に不利な立場にあるかどうかにかかわらず、「不利な立場にある」グループを特別視することは、そのグループのメンバーが良い仕事をし、それを認めてもらうことをますます難しくすることになります。

Not only must the standards be held and upheld in common but they must also be applied fairly — that is, there must be no conditions with respect to persons or groups. There must be no discrimination for or against any person for any reason. The quality of the individual performer is the issue, not the category of the performer. The aim is to recognize, reward, and promote good work. Special pleading for "disadvantaged" groups— whether disadvantaged by history, economics, or education — can only make it increasingly difficult for members of that group to do good work and have it recognized.

VI
「文学」を読むということ

42)

もし大学の教員集団が、芸術の知識と科学の知識を、相互に、また大学全体に対して、どのように学内的に配置するかという問いに答えることができなかったとしたら、その教員集団はまた、これらの知識を、真実に対して、また世界に対して、どのように対外的に配置するかという問いを立てることも出来ないでしょう。もちろん、これは危うい問いであり、私は適度な恐れをもってこの問いを提起します。このような問いは、どのようなものであれ機関によって**解決される**べきですが、しかし、それはその機関に属する人々のするべき仕事であって、機関そのものの仕事ではありません。私がここで反対しているのは、大学の専門家がキャリア準備やその手続きに没頭することに対してです。それは、教えられ、学ばれたことの真実の問題や、同様に世界における知識の行く末や利用に必要不可欠な関心を壊すからです。

If the university faculties have failed to answer the question of the internal placement of the knowledges of the arts and sciences with respect to each other and to the university as a whole, they have, it seems to me, also failed to ask the question of the external placement of these knowledges with respect to truth and to the world. This, of course, is a dangerous question, and I raise it with appropriate fear. The danger is that such questions should be **settled** by any institution whatever; these questions are the proper business of the people in the institutions, not of the institutions as such. I am arguing here against the specialist absorption in career and procedure that destroys what I take to be the indispensable interest in the question of the truth of what is taught and learned, as well as the equally indispensable interest in the fate and the use of knowledge in the world.

43)

どこかの大学が突然、「真実とは何か」という問いに活発な関心を持ち、それをどうやら教授陣の投票によって決定している最中だと聞いたら、私は驚愕するでしょう。しかし私は、大学の教員が個人的にこの問題に関心を示さないという流行にも同じような怖れを感じています。私は、この無関心が、「客観性」という名の下に、公共の美徳とされるに及んで、さらに恐ろしさが募ります。

I would be frightened to hear that some university had suddenly taken a lively interest in the question of what is true and was in the process of answering it, perhaps by a faculty vote. But I am equally frightened by the fashionable lack of interest in the question among university teachers individually. I am more frightened when this disinterest, under the alias of "objectivity," is given the status of a public virtue.

44)

客観性とは、実際には、自分のテーマ**そのもの**を、他のテーマや世界との関係には関心を持たずに研究したり教えたりすることです。つまり、その真実にはこだわらないということです。もし、人が何かの真偽を気にかけるならば、その人は客観的でいることはできません。それが真であれば喜び、偽であれば残念に思い、真と判断されれば信じ、偽であると判断されれば信じません。また、物事の真偽は、客観的に実証できないものであり、感覚や外観、直感や経験によって判断するしかありません。そして、この判断の働きは、一つの物や一つのテーマだけでは、まったく起こりません。真実の問題は、あるものと別のものとの比較から、また、あるものと他のもの、あるものと他の多くのものとの関係や影響を研究することから生まれます。

Objectivity, in practice, means that one studies or teaches one's subject **as such**, without concern for its relation to other subjects or to the world - that is, without concern for its truth. If one is concerned, if one cares, about the truth or falsity of anything, one cannot be objective: one is glad if it is true and sorry if it is false; one believes it if it is judged to be true and disbelieves it if it is judged to be false. Moreover, the truth or falsity of some things cannot be objectively demonstrated, but must be determined by feeling and appearance, intuition and experience. And this work of judgment cannot take place at all with respect to one thing or one subject alone. The issue of truth rises out of the comparison of one thing with another, out of the study of the relations and influence between one thing and another and between one thing and many others.

45)

したがって、もし教師が客観性という学術的美徳を目指すならば、教師は自分のテーマがそれ自体を超えたものとは何の関係もないかのように教えなければなりません。例えば、文学の教師は、現代の恵まれた私たちとは異なり、測定可能な証明の対象とならないものを信じた人々が残した遺物として、詩作品(poem)(訳注)の研究を提案しなければなりません。つまり、宗教詩は、かつて信じられていたが、今は信じられなくなった事柄に関係するものとして教えることができます。詩(poetry)は、詩に**ついて**学ぶべきものであり、詩**から**何かを学ぶことは、客観性を裏切る恥ずべき行いとなります。

訳注　poemは数えられる可算名詞なので詩作品とし、poetryは不可算名詞なので総称としての詩とした。

Thus, if teachers aspire to the academic virtue of objectivity, they must teach as if their subject has nothing to do with anything beyond itself. The teacher of literature, for example, must propose the study of poems as relics left by people who, unlike our highly favored modern selves, believed in things not subject to measurable proof; religious poetry, that is, may be taught as having to do with matters once believed but not believable. The poetry is to be learned **about**; to learn **from** it would be an embarrassing betrayal of objectivity.

46)

これが単なる授業のテクニックの問題ではないことは、公立学校での聖書教育をめぐる現在の騒動で十分に明らかになっています。バージニア州ブリストルにある連邦地方裁判所のジャクソン・カイザー判事は最近、公立学校の生徒に聖書を教えることは、そのコースが選択科目として提供され、「客観的な方法で教えられ、聖書の内容の真偽について子供たちを教化しようとする試みがなされない」場合に限り、合憲であると判断しました。ジェームズ・J・キルパトリックは、あるコラムでこの判決を肯定的に論じ、「シェークスピアが教えられているように」聖書が教えられてもよいと提案し、「聖書は引喩、例示、引用の宝庫である」ので、これは良い判決だと述べています。彼は「プロパガンダ［訳注：政治的、宗教的意図を持つ宣伝］と教育を分ける線は、揺れ動く砂の上に引かれた揺らぐ線である」と警告し、最後に「聖書がなんであるかは別にして、聖書は実際には文学である。そのように教えるのがコツなのだ」と強く主張しています。

That this is more than a matter of classroom technique is made sufficiently evident in the current fracas over the teaching of the Bible in public schools. Judge Jackson Kiser of the federal district court in Bristol, Virginia, recently ruled that it would be constitutional to teach the Bible to public school students if the course is offered as an elective and "taught in an objective manner with no attempt made to indoctrinate the children as to either the truth or falsity of the biblical materials." James J. Kilpatrick, who discussed this ruling approvingly in one of his columns, suggested that the Bible might be taught "as Shakespeare is taught" and that this would be good because "the Bible is a rich lode of allusion, example and quotation." He warned that "The line that divides propaganda from instruction is a wavering line drawn on shifting sands," and he concluded by asserting that "Whatever else the Bible may be, the Bible is in fact literature. The trick is to teach it that way." (5)

原注5. "Plan to Teach the Bible as Literature May Wind up in the Supreme Court," **Courier-Journal** (Louisville, Ky.) 15 Sept. 1983.

47)

ここで興味深いのは、英語話者の若者が聖書を知っているべきかどうかということではなく（もちろん知るべきですが）、私たちが信じるか信じないかに直接関係する書物を「文学として」教えることができるかどうかということです。それは明らかに、聖書の非常に本質的な部分「それが何であれ」を無視する以外には、聖書を文学として教えることはできません。そこで問題は、聖書を聖書でないものとして適切に、あるいは有益に教えることができるかどうかです。事実、聖書の著者は、カイザー判事やキルパトリック氏が「文学」と呼ぶものを書いているとは考えていませんでした。彼らは、ある人には信じられ、ある人には信じられないことを予想して、真実を書いていると考えていたのです。聖書が真実であると信じている教師、真実ではないと信じている教師、部分的に真実であると信じている教師のいずれもが、聖書を正しく教えることができると考えられます。聖書の真実の問題に関心のない教師が、聖書をうまく教えることができるとは考えられません。聖書の真実の問題に無関心な教師が何世代にもわたって、聖書への生き生きとした関心を保ち続けることもまた考えられません。

The interesting question here is not whether young English speakers should know the Bible — they obviously should — but whether a book that so directly offers itself to our belief or disbelief can be taught "as literature." It clearly cannot be so taught except by ignoring "whatever else [it] may be," which is a very substantial part of it. The question, then, is whether it can be adequately or usefully taught as something less than it is. The fact is that the writers of the Bible did not think that they were writing what Judge Kiser and Mr. Kilpatrick call "literature." They thought they were writing the truth, which they expected to be believed by some and disbelieved by others. It is conceivable that the Bible could be well taught by a teacher who believes that it is true, by a teacher who believes that it is untrue, or by a teacher who believes that it is partly true. That it could be well taught by a teacher uninterested in the question of its truth is not conceivable. That a lively interest in the Bible could be maintained through several generations of teachers uninterested in the question of its truth is also not conceivable.

48)

明らかに、この公立学校における聖書の問題は、教育方法を規定する連邦裁判所の判決では解決できるものではありません。それは、教師の信念に基づいて教える自由と、教師や学校と地域社会との関係という観点においてのみ解決できるものです。今回の論争では、地域社会の崩壊の必然的な結果として、公立学校制度の崩壊を目の当たりにしているのかもしれません。この問題を裁判で解決できるとは到底思えません。

訳注　ここでの著者ウェンデル・ベリーの主張は、共同体主義（コミュニタリアニズム）に近い。すなわち、共同体の構成員はある程度共通の価値観（例えばアメリカの場合、キリスト教や民主主義等）を共有していることが共同体にとって望ましい、とする議論である。

Obviously, this issue of the Bible in the public schools cannot be resolved by federal court decisions that prescribe teaching methods. It can only be settled in terms of the freedom of teachers to teach as they believe and in terms of the relation of teachers and schools to their local communities. It may be that in this controversy we are seeing the breakdown of the public school system, as an inevitable consequence of the breakdown of local communities. It is hard to believe that this can be remedied in courts of law.

49)

とにかく私が言いたいのは、私たちが文学を「文学として」すでに教えているのでなければ、つまりそれが真実であろうとなかろうと私たちがまったく気にせず、どうでもよいことであるかのようにすでに教えているのでなければ、私たちは聖書を「文学として」教えることは考えられなかったということです。このような事態を招いた原因は数多くあります。中でも顕著なのは、文学をはじめとする「人文学」の教師たちが、自分たちの真実が科学の真実のように客観的に証明できるものではないということを恥じていることが大きいと思われます。現在、経験や想像力、感情や信仰に確証の根拠をおいた主張には、恥ずかしさがあります。そして、この恥ずかしさは、そのような主張を単に人工物、文化的遺物、歴史的証拠の一部、あるいは「美的価値」のあるものとして扱おうとする圧倒的な衝動を生み出しています。つまり、私たちは研究し、記録し、分析し、批判し、評価します。しかし、私たちはそれらを信じることはなく、完全な意味で知ることはありません。

My point, anyhow, is that we could not consider teaching the Bible "as literature" if we were not already teaching literature "as literature" — as if we do not care, as if it does not matter, whether or not it is true. The causes of this are undoubtedly numerous, but prominent among them is a kind of shame among teachers of literature and other "humanities" that their truths are not objectively provable as are the truths of science. There is now an embarrassment about any statement that depends for confirmation upon experience or imagination or feeling or faith, and this embarrassment has produced an overwhelming impulse to treat such statements merely as artifacts, cultural relics, bits of historical evidence, or things of "aesthetic value." We will study, record, analyze, criticize, and appreciate. But we will not believe; we will not, in the full sense, know.

50)

その結果、多くの教師、歴史家、文学批評家は「批判的客観性」というスタンスをとるようになります。数学者や化学者のようにではありませんが（つまり彼らの方法論はまだ使えないので）、まるで動物行動学者のように、自分が属していない種の行動を研究し、その歴史や運命に関与せず、自分自身のために何かを知るのではなく、「知識を促進する」ことを目的としてしまうのです。これは、テキストの構造的理解の仕方としては有効かもしれませんが、それは偉大な文学作品を知るためのアプローチではありません。その方法は、単純に「彼ら」が「当時」何を考えていたかに興味を持つ人たちには閉ざされています。また、「ダンテの世界」や「シェイクスピアの世界」が「我々の世界」とはかけ離れていてまったく異質であると考える人たちにも閉ざされており、さらに詩的な仕掛けや感情的な効果、審美的な価値を考える人たちにも閉ざされています。

訳注　ダンテ(1265-1321)イタリアの詩人、政治家。『神曲』(1321)を著した。

The result is a stance of "critical objectivity" that causes many teachers, historians, and critics of literature to sound — not like mathematicians or chemists: their methodology does not permit that yet — but like ethologists, students of the behavior of a species to which they do not belong, in whose history and fate they have no part, their aim being, not to know anything for themselves, but to "advance knowledge." This may be said to work, as a textual mechanics, but it is not an approach by which one may know any great work of literature. That route is simply closed to people interested in what "they" thought "then" ; it is closed to people who think that "Dante's world" or "Shakespeare's world" is far removed and completely alienated from "our world" ; and it is closed to the viewers of poetic devices, emotional effects, and esthetic values.

51)

近代文学の運命の背後にある大きな困惑は、次のようなコールリッジの主張に表現されていると私は思います。彼は『抒情歌謡集』を書いた時の自分の努力は、「私たちの内なる本性から……十分な真実らしさの感覚を伝えるためであり、さらにその目的は、それら想像力の影像に、不信の念の自発的な一時停止を起こさせるためであって、これこそが詩的信仰そのものです」と言っています（訳注）。それは、震えとおののきに満ちた文章です。私たちの内なる本性は、見かけだけで真実なのでしょうか？ 芸術作品において、真実と「真実の見かけ」との間には、どのような違いがあるのでしょうか？ 「詩的信仰」を他の種類の信仰から切り離し、また「詩的信仰」を意志に依存させると、どのような結果になるのでしょうか？

訳注 サミュエル・コールリッジ(1772-1834)は、英国の詩人、批評家。ワーズワースと共に、ロマン主義の金字塔ともいうべき詩集『抒情歌謡集』(1798)を生み出した。有名な『老水夫の歌』はこの詩集の巻頭を飾る。

The great distraction behind the modern fate of literature, I think, is expressed in Coleridge's statement that his endeavor in **Lyrical Ballads** was "to transfer from our inward nature ... a semblance of truth sufficient to procure for these shadows of imagination that willing suspension of disbelief for the moment, which constitutes poetic faith." (6) That is a sentence full of quakes and tremors. Is our inward nature true only by semblance? What is the difference, in a work of art, between truth and "semblance of truth"? What must be the result of separating "poetic faith" from faith of any other kind and then of making "poetic faith" dependent upon will?

原注6. Samuel Coleridge, **Biographia Literaria**, chapter 14.

52)

問題の本質は、**意志的な**という形容詞にあります。この形容詞は、信じられるものに対する信じる者の優位性を暗示します。この暗示は、まったくの偽りと私は確信しています。信じることは意志に先行します。人は信じるか信じないかのどちらかであり、もし信じるのであれば、人は進んで信じます。もし信じないのであれば、たとえそれが不本意であっても、世界中のどんな意志も人を信じさせることはできません。信じることは自由意志によらない（無意識的な）ものであり、老水夫が海蛇の美しさと神聖さを認識したのと同じです。

愛の泉が心に溢れて、
思わずわしは彼らを讃えた……。(訳注)

訳注　ワーズワス、コールリッジ『抒情歌謡集』より「第四部 老水夫の歌」宮下忠二訳、大修館書店、1984年、16頁。コールリッジは、人が詩を読むときには、常識的に考えれば現実にはありそうもないこともあり得るものとして自然に受け入れることができるようになり、「真実らしさの感覚」が引き出される、と考えた。詩人の想像力が読者をひとときそのような心の状態にさせるのである。「不信の念の自発的な一時停止」は、言い換えれば読者が自ら進んで想像力の世界に入ることであり、これを彼は「詩的信仰」の状態と呼ぶ。この「老水夫の詩」は、読者をまさにその「詩的信仰」の世界に誘うものとして書かれている。（参考『文学的自叙伝』、同書訳者解説）

The gist of the problem is in that adjective **willing**, which implies the superiority of the believer to what is believed. This implication, I am convinced, is simply untrue. Belief precedes will. One either believes or one does not, and, if one believes, then one willingly believes. If one disbelieves, even unwillingly, all the will in the world cannot make one believe. Belief is involuntary, as is the Ancient Mariner's recognition of the beauty and sanctity of the water snakes:

A spring of love gushed from my heart,
And I blessed them unaware ...

53)

この自由意志によらない信こそが、偉大な著作物への唯一のアプローチなのです。もちろん、信じないこともありうるため、信じない人が信じない人として読み、批評する権利を認めなければなりません。なぜならば、信じないことは正当な反応であり、起こり得る反応だからです。私たちは、信をおくことが間違っているかもしれないという可能性を認識し、間違った信から目覚める必要があることを認識しなければなりません。つまり、「深淵に足を踏み入れるように、信に足を踏み入れる必要はありません」。しかし、信じないということは、実は作品の外にいるということでもあることを意識しなければなりません。作品の**中にいる**ときは、信じるかどうかについて自分自身と議論する可能性はとっくに終わっています。作品の**中にいる**と、偉大なるオデュッセウス(訳注1)が帰ってきたこと、ダンテが天空の薔薇の前にいること、コーデリアが父親に抱かれているが死んでしまったこと(訳注2)、などを、私たちは単純に**知ってい**ます。これらのことを知っていれば、マグダラのマリアが復活したキリストを庭師と間違えたこともわかるはずです(訳注3)。そしてその結果として、客観的な学者には軽視され、連邦判事からは修正される対象となる可能性があります。

訳注1　オデュッセウス　ホメロスの叙事詩『オデュッセイア』(紀元前6世紀頃成立)の主人公。
訳注2　コーデリア　シェークスピア『リア王』(1606)の登場人物。主人公リア王の末娘。
訳注3　マグダラのマリア　『新約聖書』中の福音書に出てくる、イエスに従っていた女性の一人。

This involuntary belief is the only approach to the great writings. One may, assuredly, not believe, and we must, of course, grant unbelievers the right to read and comment as unbelievers, for disbelief is a legitimate response, because it is a possible one. We must be aware of the possibility that belief may be false, and of the need to awaken from false belief; "one need not step into belief as into an abyss." (7) But we must be aware also that to disbelieve is to remain, in an important sense, outside the work. When we are **in** the work, we are long past the possibility of any debate with ourselves about whether or not to be willing to believe. When we are **in** the work, we simply **know** that great Odysseus has come home, that Dante is in the presence of the celestial rose, that Cordelia, though her father carries her in his arms, is dead. If we know these things, we are apt to know too that Mary Magdalene mistook the risen Christ for the gardener — and are thus eligible to be taken lightly by objective scholars, and to be corrected by a federal judge.

原注7.　Harry Mason, in a letter to the author.

54)

私たちとこれらの作品は想像力の中で出会い、想像力によって私たちはその真実を知るのです。想像力においては、宗教的な信仰がないのと同様に、「詩的な信仰」というものも存在しません。信はどこで起きても同じであり、その条件は常に想像力によって設定されます。人は**見る**から信じるのであって、情報に基づいて信じるのではありません。だからこそ、コペルニクスから400年経った今でも、「太陽が昇っている」と言い続けているのです。

We and these works meet in imagination; by imagination we know their truth. In imagination, there is no specifically or exclusively "poetic faith," just as there is no faith that is specifically or exclusively religious. Belief is the same wherever it happens, and its terms are invariably set by the imagination. One believes, that is, because one **sees**, not because one is informed. That is why, four hundred years after Copernicus, we still say, "The sun is rising."

55)

私たちが「サー・パトリック・スペンス」というバラッド（物語詩）を読むとき、騎士とその部下が溺れたことを知るのは、「彼らの帽子が水の上を漂っていた」からであって、歴史的文書の研究によってその出来事を確認したからではありません。そして、「サー・パトリック」のバラッドよりもはるかに奇妙なトーマス・ライマーのバラッド(訳注)にも合意せざるを得ないとしたら、私たちはどうすればいいのでしょうか？信じて詩の世界に入り、公式記録にもなく、新聞でもそのような話を読んだことがなく、自分の経験でもそのようなことを知らないからといって、不信の念を持って詩の世界から引き返さなければならないのでしょうか？それとも、現実は思ったよりも大きいかもしれないという証拠の一つとして、詩の力を意識しながら詩と一緒に生きていくべきでしょうか？

訳注　トーマス・ライマー(1250-1290) はイギリスの詩人。韻文のロマンス『サー・トリストレム(Sir Tristrem)』（刊行年不詳）の作者。正確な予言を行ったことでも名高い伝説的人物。

When we read the ballad of Sir Patrick Spens we know that the knight and his men have drowned because "Thair hats they swam aboone," not because we have confirmed the event by the study of historical documents. And if our assent is forced also by the ballad of Thomas Rhymer, far stranger than that of Sir Patrick, what are we to say? Must we go, believing, into the poem, and then return from it in disbelief because we find the story in no official record, have read of no such thing in the newspaper, and know nothing like it in our own experience? Or must we live with the poem, with our awareness of its power over us, as a piece of evidence that reality may be larger than we thought?

56)

「ギリシャの神々を信じていないから、ホメロス（訳注1）を正しく読むことができないのでしょうか」と聞かれたことがあります。私が答えられるのは、ホメロスを正しく読めば、必ず彼の神々を何らかの形で信じるように**なる**ということです。そうでなければ、キリスト教作家の作品の中に神々が現代まで生き残っていることを説明できないのではないでしょうか？この生き残りは、C.S.ルイスの小説『かの忌わしき砦』（訳注2）の中で、ギリシャのこの世の神々が天使として地上に再登場する最後の部分で神格化されているように私には思えます。ルイスはホメロスを読んだキリスト教徒として小説を書きましたが、明らかに、彼は、その想像力が、不信を自発的に中断させるような臨床装置には妨げられない人として読んでいたのです。そのような読者として、彼はキリスト教信者でありながら、異教の神々がある種の権威を保ち、ある種の同意を求めていることを読み取っていたのです。イギリス文学の伝統における多くの先人たちと同様に、彼は異教の神々に憧れを抱いていました。異教の神々が、『かの忌わしき砦』の最後に、キリスト教の天上の階層の一員として凱旋して戻ってくることは、必ずしも驚きではありません。それは、その小説そのものだけでなく、英文学の歴史の中に見出される解決策です。スペンサー（訳注3）やミルトン（訳注4）の亡霊が安堵のため息をついているのが聞こえてきます。

訳注1　ホメロス（紀元前8世紀頃？）はギリシアの詩人。経歴未詳。ヨーロッパ最古の詩人とよばれ、英雄叙事詩『イリアス』、前出の『オデュッセイア』などの作者とされる。

訳注2　C.S.ルイス(1898-1963)は科学者、科学精神を批判するための科学ロマンスもしくは神学的SFとしてこの作品(1945)を書いたとされる。（参考：『サルカンドラ：かの忌まわしき砦』中村妙子、西村徹訳、ちくま文庫、1987年「訳者あとがき」「解説」）

訳注3　スペンサー(Edmund Spencer)(1552頃-1559)は、エリザベス１世時代のイギリスの詩人。シェークスピアとともにイギリス・ルネサンス文学を代表し「詩人の中の詩人」といわれる。

訳注4　ミルトン(John Milton)(1608-1674)は、17世紀イギリスの詩人。神に仕える「詩人」を天職とし、『失楽園』(1667)ほか多数の著作を残した。

"Does that mean," I am asked, "that it's not possible for us to read Homer properly because we don't believe in the Greek gods?" I can only answer that I suspect that a proper reading of Homer will **result** in some manner of belief in his gods. How else explain their survival in the works of Christian writers into our own time? This survival has its apotheosis, it seems to me, in C.S. Lewis's novel, **That Hideous Strength**, at the end of which the Greek planetary deities reappear on earth as angels. Lewis wrote as a Christian who had read Homer, but he had read, obviously, as a man whose imagination was not encumbered with any such clinical apparatus as the willing suspension of disbelief. As such a reader, though he was a Christian, his reading had told him that the pagan gods retained a certain authority and commanded a certain assent. Like many of his forebears in English literary tradition, he yearned toward them. Their triumphant return, at the end of **That Hideous Strength**, as members of the heavenly hierarchy of Christianity, is not altogether a surprise. It is a profound resolution, not only in the novel itself, but in the history of English literature. One hears the ghosts of Spenser and Milton sighing with relief.

VII
想像力と
大学の産業（工業）化

57)

想像力の信頼性をめぐる疑問に、私はまだ答えを得られないままかもしれません。なぜなら、想像力はすぐに証明されたり、実証されたりするものではないからです。多くの場合、想像力は、経験によるゆっくりとした部分的な確認を必要とします。つまり、厳密ではないにせよ、想像力は、現実的に正しいことが認証され、修正されるべき対象です。想像力が生んだ作品が時を越えて存続するためには、それが根拠のあるものであることが証明され、修正にも耐えなければなりません。それは、経験や批判的判断によって、そしてさらなる想像力の働きによって修正可能です。

Questions of the authenticity of imaginings invite answers, and yet may remain unanswered. For the imagination is not always subject to immediate proof or demonstration. It is often subject only to the slow and partial authentication of experience. It is subject, that is, to a practical, though not an exact, validation, and it is subject to correction. For a work of imagination to endure through time, it must prove valid, and it must survive correction. It is correctable by experience, by critical judgment, and by further works of imagination.

58)

想像力が生んだ作品が修正を必要とすると言うことは、当然のことながら、「現実の世界」とは異なる、あるいは、対立する「想像力の世界」が存在しないことを意味します。想像力は、世界の「**中に**」あり、世界の中で働き、世界にとって必要であり、世界によって修正可能なものです。この経験による想像力の修正は、想像力によって経験を修正することと同様に、避けられないし、必要で、終わりのないものです。これこそが、私たち全員に求められている批判の重要で一般的な機能です。それは、歴史的か、農業的か、生物学的批判である以上に文学的な批判ではありませんが、それにもかかわらず、他のあらゆる種類の批判と同様に、文学的な批判の働きの基本的な部分でなければならないのです。人間の最も重要な要求の一つは、想像力の真実が世界のあらゆる生活と場所において証明されること、そしてまた、世界の生活と場所の真実が想像力の中で証明されることです。

To say that a work of imagination is subject to correction is, of course, to imply that there is no "world of imagination" as distinct from or opposed to the "real world." The imagination is **in** the world, is at work in it, is necessary to it, and is correctable by it. This correcting of imagination by experience is inescapable, necessary, and endless, as is the correcting of experience by imagination. This is the great general work of criticism to which we all are called. It is not literary criticism any more than it is historical or agricultural or biological criticism, but it must nevertheless be a fundamental part of the work of literary criticism, as it must be of criticisms of all other kinds. One of the most profound of human needs is for the truth of imagination to prove itself in every life and place in the world, and for the truth of the world's lives and places to be proved in imagination.

59)

この要求は、想像力の働き、つまり人間の作ったものを、特別なケースとして、何らかの形で世界に提供する特権を与えられているという議論から、私たちを可能な限り遠ざけます。まさにこのような議論とその結果としての一般的な批判の放棄が、大学が産業原理に基づいて組織化されることを許したのです。あたかも学部や学生、そして彼らが教えたり学んだりするものすべてが、機械の部品に過ぎないかのように、その目的を一般的に定義することも、ましてや疑問を持つこともしなかったのです。そして現在、この産業原理とその比喩が、主に大学の仲介的働きによって、私たちの自然との関係、そしてお互いの関係を支配しています。

This need takes us as far as possible from the argument for works of imagination, human artifacts, as special cases, privileged somehow to offer themselves to the world on their own terms. It is this argument and the consequent abandonment of the general criticism that have permitted the universities to organize themselves on the industrial principle, as if faculties and students and all that they might teach and learn are no more than parts of a machine, the purpose of which they have, in general, not bothered to define, much less to question. And largely through the agency of the universities, this principle and this metaphor now dominate our relation to nature and to one another.

VIII
大学が健全であるための問い

60)

大学は自らの健全さのために、教えていることが真実かどうかの問題に関心を持たなければなりません。そして世界の健全さのために、大学はその真実なるものが世界でどのような運命をたどるか、そしてその真実なるものが世界でどのように使われるかに関心を持たなければなりません。大学は、卒業生がどこに住み、どこで働き、何をしているのかを知りたいと思わなければなりません。卒業生は、故郷に帰り、自らの知識で近隣の人々の生活を向上させ、守ったりしているのでしょうか？卒業生は、今現在、全国各地の人間・自然を含めた地域社会で搾取・破壊を専門とする「上昇志向」集団への仲間入りをしているのでしょうか。この一世代で、大学は、古典の読み書き能力や知識を高めたのでしょうか、それとも落としたのでしょうか。科学の一般的な理解を、高めることが出来たのでしょうか。公害や土壌侵食の増加と減少は、どうなっているのでしょうか。公務員の真実を語る能力や意欲を高めたのでしょうか、あるいは落としたのでしょうか。もちろん、このような問いは、正確に答えられるものではありません。しかし、大学の影響力に関する質問は、決して問えないものではありません。それらは問うことができるものであり、そして、もし私たちが問うことを選ぶなら、その問いは、大学を統一する力となり、大学を創造する力となるはずです。

If, for the sake of its own health, a university must be interested in the question of the truth of what it teaches, then, for the sake of the world's health, it must be interested in the fate of that truth and the uses made of it in the world. It must want to know where its graduates live, where they work, and what they do. Do they return home with their knowledge to enhance and protect the life of their neighborhoods? Do they join the "upwardly mobile" professional force now exploiting and destroying local communities, both human and natural, all over the country? Has the work of the university over the last generation, increased or decreased literacy and knowledge of the classics? Has it increased or decreased the general understanding of the sciences? Has it increased or decreased pollution and soil erosion? Has it increased or decreased the ability and the willingness of public servants to tell the truth? Such questions are not, of course, precisely answerable. Questions about influence never are. But they are askable, and the asking, should we choose to ask, would be a unifying and a shaping force.

訳注は主に以下を参照：

『岩波 哲学・思想事典』岩波書店、1998年

『ブリタニカ国際大百科事典』小項目電子辞書版、ブリタニカジャパン、2012年

『旺文社世界史事典 三訂版』https://kotobank.jp/dictionary/obunshasekaishi/、最終閲覧日2022年10月31日

『20世紀西洋人名事典』日外アソシエーツ、1995年
https://kotobank.jp/dictionary/western20/、最終閲覧日2022年10月31日

原典：Berry, Wendell (1987). "The loss of the University", in *Home Economics*, pp.76-97, North Point Press.

訳者あとがき

なぜ今、詩人ウェンデル・ベリーの教育論なのか！

本書は、ウェンデル・ベリーのエッセー Wendell Berry, “The Loss of the University”, in *Home Economics* pp76-97, North Point Press, 1987. の翻訳である。*Home Economics* は 14 本のエッセーからなる著作で、“The Loss of the University” はその 6 番目のエッセーである。エッセーは年代順に並べられており、最初のエッセー “Letter to Wes Jackson” は 1982 年、中程の “The Loss of the University” は 1984 年、最後の “Does Community Have Value” は 1986 年に書かれている。すなわち、“The Loss of the University” は、約 40 年前に書かれたものであるにもかかわらず、そこに「古さ」を感じることはなかった。ベリーの前書きによれば、これらのエッセーは、それぞれの前のエッセーを受けて書かれたとのことだ。“The Loss of the University” の前にあるエッセーは “Two Economies (1983)” で、それは加藤貞通訳『ウェンデル・ベリーの環境思想』昭和堂 2008 の「7 章 二つの経済」に掲載されている。二つの経済とは、自然の「大経済」と人間の「小経済」のことである。人間は、大経済（生態系：包括的で宗教的）のなかでしか生きる場所を持たないので、個人は大経済を大切にしながら小経済、地域と「家庭の経済」、に責任を持ってより良く運営しなければならない。この意味で本のタイトルが *Home Economics* となっている。詳しくは、「二つの経済」を参照していただきたい。

ウェンデル・ベリーは、1934 年 8 月 5 日にケンタッキー州ヘンリー郡で四人の子供の長男としてタバコ栽培農家に生まれた。現在 (2023.1.1)、88 歳。父親は、弁護士で農業従事者でもあった。ベリーは、1955 年にケンタッキー大学、英文学で学士号、1957 年に修士号を取得した。同年、ターニャ・アミクスと結婚。1958年、ベリーはステグナー奨学金を得て、スタンフォード大学の著名な作家W. ステグナーの下で創作を学んだ。1961年、グッケンハイム助成金により、ベリーは家族と共にイタリアとフランスで暮らした。1962-63年、ニューヨーク大学で英語を教え、1964年にケンタッキー大学に移り、創作を教えたが1977年に大学を辞職した。1977-80年、ペンシルベニア州ロデール社の『Organic Gardening and Farming』『The New Farm』などの編集と執筆を担当。1987-93年、ケンタッキー大学の英語学科に戻り英語・英文学を教えた。

1965年7月4日、ベリーと妻、二人の子供は、故郷ヘンリー郡ポートロイヤルの近く（Lanes Landing）、12エーカーの農場に移り、最終的に約117エーカー(47 ha)の場所でトウモロコシと小粒穀物を育て始めた。以来、ベリーはレーズ・ランディング農場で農業を営み、居住し、執筆活動を続けている。合衆国でベリーは、詩人、小説家、活動家、環境保護活動家、農夫としてよく知られているが、その仕事のすべてにおいて長けていることから、「ルネサンス人」とも呼ばれている。（文末に示した、ベリーの三つの訳書　1）『言葉と立場』、2)『ライフ・イズ・ミラクル』3)『ウェンデル・ベリーの環境思想』、と合衆国のwikiなどを参照にした）。

翻訳は、私（魚類生物学を専門）が中部大学に赴任（2011）し、新しい15回の講義「環境問題入門」を準備する過程でウェンデル・ベリーの著作を知ったことから始まった。私は、J. ベニュス（1987）『自然と生体に学ぶバイオミミクリー』（2006, 山本良一監訳、吉野美耶子訳、オーム社）を読み、生物が持つ進化的な適応技術を人間の技術に模倣応用するというバイオミミクリー（bio＝生物＋mimicry=模倣）を講義の中に組み込んだ。ベニュスは、その本の序文の謝辞に「……バイオミミクリーの持つ意味を明確に慎重に考えてきたウェンデル・ベリーから受けた恩恵は大きいものでした」と記していた。そこで、バイオミミクリーをもっと知るために、ウェンデル・ベリーの訳書３冊を読んだ。驚いたことに、ベリーの著作は、バイオミミクリーを説明する本とは違いその３冊は、ベリーの「生態学的な世界観・生命観」を主張するものであった。

『言葉と立場』の巻頭文にある津田塾大元教授のD. ラミス氏は、「ウェンデル・ベリーのこと」について解説している。「農夫であると同時にベリーは詩人であり、小説家であり、文芸評論家である。また、生態環境についての彼の本は合衆国でもっとも敬意を払って読まれているもののひとつである。彼は専門家になることを拒んだが、そのためかえってその作品のすべてが、専門家には望めない深い味わいを持つにいたった。つまり、ウェンデル・ベリーは彼の言葉を守っているのだ。ほとんどの作家……とは異なって、ベリーは実行すべきだと主張することを自ら実践している。彼の作品と人生は、私たちが生きる時代を反駁しているのだ。彼こそは、今世紀には存在し得ないと思われるような人である。詩を描き、スペンサー（英国の哲学者 1820-1903）とポープ（英国の詩人 1688-1744）を読み、馬を使って耕す農夫が今世紀に存在すると、一体誰に考えることができようか。次から次へと著書を出版し、なおワープロを拒否するような作家が。経済成長と原子力に反対し、その論拠を英文学の古典に置くような保守論者が。彼は他の時代からきた人間にちがいない。一九世紀の遺物などと呼ぶ人もあろう。だが、私は楽観的な見方を好む。だから言おう、彼は二十一世紀の人間なのだと」。つまり、ベリーは、日本であまり知られていないが合衆国では著名人なのだ。

ベリーの３冊の訳書はどれも見事な訳文であった。難解なベリー文章の訳出にはご苦労が伴ったと想像される。谷恵理子氏は訳者あとがきで、「ごく身近なものから宇宙の思考の存在までも捉えようとする貪欲なまでの著者の姿勢に、ともすればふり回されそうになりながらの翻訳であった。どんなに努力はしても浅学非才の身、不明の点が多々あった」と書かれている。同感である。友人である、加藤貞通氏の訳者あとがき「落ち着きを失いゆく時代に」から、ベリーのアグラリアン（農的生活者）としての合衆国での位置づけを学ぶことができた。

『ライフ・イズ・ミラクル』の訳者の三国千秋氏は、そのあとがきで「教育」について色々と考えることができたと、次のように記している。「高い学力や学歴はそれ自体として価値あるかもしれないが、それは一部の人々にとって価値のあるものであり、すべての人間にとって価値あるものではないであろう。……『高学力』を教育の本質とみなすことから問題が生じてくる。……とりわけ『高学力』や「社会的上昇志向」といった価値観から排除される若者は、大きな失望を味わうことになる」。「だとしたら、われわれは教育においても、今一度「生命」であることに立ち返る必要があるだろう。生命を機械とみなすことを止め、教育の内容とあり方を機械的効率や経済効率によって判断することの誤りに気づくべきである。大人がまず子供たちに教えるべきは、生命を大切にすることである。そのためには、大人が生命の大切さやコミュニティの健全さに気づかねばならない」。ベリーの "The Loss of the University" を知ったのも三国氏の熱のこもったあとがきによってであった。

私は、中部大学応用生物学部長を務めた３年間（2015-7)、また國分前副学長（ものつくり大学学長）と取り組んだ大学院の新プログラム（持続社会創成プログラム）を考えた４年間（2018-21)、いつも "The Loss of the University" を教育の中心に考えていた。生物学を専門にする、私にとってそれは、教育への手引きであった。2022 年の 4 月に中部大学の客員教授となった機会に "The Loss of the University" の翻訳を本格的に開始した。翻訳は粗訳が出来上がったが理解できないところが多くあったので、文理融合で翻訳にあたることにした。翻訳は、"The Loss of the University" の中身がリベラル・アーツであることから、大学院の新プログラムで「文理融合」科目を担当する鈴木順子先生（創造的リベラルアーツセンター副センター長）とで行った。現代教育の三島浩路先生（現代教育学部長）には教育学の立場からの解説をいただいた。太田明徳先生（中部大学総長補佐）と杉本和弘先生（中部大学学長顧問）にそれぞれのご専門からの丁寧な数多いコメントとアドバイスをいただいた。また、中高研の福井弘道所長から施設の利用の許可をいただいた、記してお礼申し上げる。

今は、危機的な気候変動があり、長引くパンデミックがあり、終わる目処の立たないウクライナ戦争もあり、まさに混迷の時代である。また、社会はグローバル経済と「今だけ、金だけ、自分だけ」の新自由主義経済の真只中にある。

こんな時代であるからこそ、よりよい社会に向かうために大学の役割が問われるべきなのかもしれない。また、こんな時代だからこそ社会を根元から問いかける詩人の教育論を読む機会があっても良いのかもしれない。本書が、学生と直接対面する大学の現場で活躍する先生方に少しでもお役に立つならば、訳者は望外の喜びである。

謝辞

翻訳許可に関しては、著者の Wendell Berry 氏、Counterpoint Press の Jack Shoemaker 氏と The Wendell Berry Center の Ben Aguilar 氏にご援助いただきました。また写真に関して、Ben Aguilar 氏の未公開写真を利用させていただきました。記してお礼申し上げます。

ベリーの翻訳書

1) *Standing by Words* (1983), North Point Press:『言葉と立場』谷恵理子訳、マルジュ社、1995

2) *Life is a miracle: An Against Modern Superstition* (2000), Counterpoint:『ライフ・イズ・ミラクル』三国千秋訳、法政大学出版局、2005

3) *The Art of the Commonplace: The Agrarian Essays of Wendell Berry*, ed. by N. Wirzba (2002), Counterpoint:『ウェンデル・ベリーの環境思想(抄訳)』加藤貞通訳、昭和堂、2008

宗宮弘明

解説

「大学の喪失：その再生への希望」を読む

現代教育学部（学部長）　三島浩路

小学校から高等学校まで、日本の学校で教育する内容は学習指導要領に定められている。一方、大学での教育は、教員の専門性にもとづき、教育内容をある程度柔軟に設定することができる。大学教員が教える内容は、教員の専門性にもとづいているが、それぞれの分野の専門性が高まることにより、専門分野を異にする教員間のコミュニケーションが難しくなり、「大学自身の統一性を失うことになります」と著者は述べている。

本書の読後感として、教員間のコミュニケーションが専門性の高い壁に阻まれ機能不全に陥った大学の姿が、枝葉ばかりが大きく広がり、その枝葉を細い幹が頼りなく支える姿として浮かぶ。

ところで、大学に入学したばかりの学生は、多くの場合、自分が大学で学び探求する分野について、専門的な知識をほとんどもっていない。そうした青年の専門性を高め、学士・修士、さらには博士の学位をもつ専門家を養成することは大学の重要な使命である。しかし、大学に入学した多くの青年が研究者などの専門家になるわけではない。むしろ、大部分は、大学での学びに若干関連がある生業を得て社会人となり、その後の長い人生を歩む。こうした大学の現状を意識の片隅に起き、はじめに、大学が行う教育について著者の考えに触れてみたい。

近年、大学教育を受けるために必要な学力をもっていない入学生の存在が問題視され、こうした学生のために、高校レベルの授業を大学が行うこともある。この点について著者は、「それは、高校から高校がやるべきことを取り除き、高校を楽にさせるだけであり、その過程で大学は自分の義務を果たせなくなります」と、その問題点を指摘する。また、学生生活の出口である就職を意識したキャリア（準備）教育についても著者は、「『キャリア準備』教育は、雇用者の監督下での見習い期間中に最も効率よく、適切に習得されるものなので、それはまた、学生の時間の浪費」と手厳しく否定的である。

それでは、著者が考える教育とはどのようなものか。大学教員が研究者として行う研究や教育など、大学の在り方全般について、本書に登場する「幹」と「枝」というメタファーを用いて、著者の考えを私なりに整理してみたい。

高度な専門性により細分化された知識を「枝」に、専門性の根底にある万物の原理を「幹」にたとえ、いくつもの枝を幹から伸ばすことはできるが、枝から幹を伸ばすことは難しいと述べるなど、「幹」や「枝」という言葉に込められた著者の考えはいくつもの階層をもっており、本書を包括する対立的なメタファーといえよう。

大学教育における本来の課題は、いかに解りやすく話し、書くかであって、ジャーナリストやビジネス英語の実践者などに、どのようにしてなるのかということではないと著者が述べた部分は、大学教育の「幹」と「枝」を例示したものであろう。また、大学教育における課題に関しても、「幹」と「枝」の関係を思わせる次のような例示がある。それは、「作文コース」の授業だけで学生の文作力や質を評価し、「歴史」などの他の授業ではこうした点の評価は除外され、内容のみが評価される場合、文作力や質は「作文コース」の授業でのみ重要であり、実際にはほとんど重要ではないという誤ったメッセージを学生に伝えているというものだ。「作文コース」「歴史」などといった個々の授業の独立性のみが尊重され、授業をとおして実現される大学教育全体の統一性が損なわれる危うさの例示とも読み取れる。

「幹」と「枝」のメタファーは、大学教育に関する記述に留まらず、学問そのものの在り方に対する著者の主張にもかかわる。専門的になり過ぎたそれぞれの学問と、大学自身の統一性の基盤となる共通の言語は、「枝」と「幹」との関係にあり、「共通の言葉がなければ、大学は教育への関心を失うだけでなく、大学自身の統一性をも失うことになります」と著者は述べる。そして、「大学の崩壊が専門家重視のイデオロギーから始まるとすれば、それは顧客を満足させようとする商業的な強制力によって強化されることになります」と、その社会的な背景にも言及している。

「幹」と「枝」との対立的なメタファーは本書の中で重層的に展開し、聖書と「客観性」をあつかった部分で深部へと至る。

キリスト教徒の信仰の書として聖書は英語をはじめとした様々な言語に翻訳され読み継がれてきた。合衆国の公立学校の教材として聖書を利用することについて、「聖書は隠喩、例示、引用の豊富な鉱脈である」として、「客観的な方法で教えられ、聖書の内容の真偽について子供たちを教化しようとする試みがなされない」場合に限り、聖書を公立学校の生徒に教えることは合憲という判断を合衆国連邦地方裁判所は下した。この判断について、信仰の書である聖書の本質ではない隠喩・例示など、いわゆる「枝」の部分を重視するもと著者はとらえているようであり、その背景にある「客観性という学問的美徳」について述べている。そして、「文学をはじめとする『人文学』の教師たちが、自分たちの真実が科学の真実のように客観的に証明できるものではないということを恥じている」と述べ、「客観性という学問的美徳」についての再考を促しているように読み取れる。

著者の主張はキャリア（準備）教育や学問分野の専門性重視といった「枝」部分が、社会的な要請などにより重視される現状を、「現代の大学は、切り落とされた枝が無造作に宙を舞っているような状態」と批判的に捉え、“university”という語に託されたすべての学問を統合するという大学の理念に立ち返り、「共通の言葉で誰にでもわかりやすく話さねばならないという不可避な義務」の実現を求めるものとなっている。

「共通の言葉」は本書の重要語である。専門化した学問分野を牽引する研究者がその研究を「わかりやすく話す」ことは、大学の発展だけでなく人類の英知の深化にも貢献する。ところで、専門化した学問分野を牽引する研究者に求めるものが、「わかりやすく話す」ことであるとするなら、その話を聞きインスピレーションを膨らます我々に必要なものはなんだろうか。本書で展開された「枝」と「幹」の何層にもなる物語から、自分の研究や教育についてもう一度、見つめ直してみたい。

鈴木順子（すずき　じゅんこ）
1965年生まれ。東京大学大学院総合文化研究科地域文化研究専攻博士課程単位取得満期退学。学術博士。フランス・ポワティエ大学大学院人文科学部哲学科DEA（哲学史）取得。
中部大学創造的リベラルアーツセンター教授。専門分野：フランス思想・哲学、フランス地域文化。
単著：『シモーヌ・ヴェイユ 「歓び」の思想』藤原書店（2023）、『シモーヌ・ヴェイユ 「犠牲」の思想』藤原書店（2012）、共著：『リベラルアーツと自然科学』水声社（2023）など。

宗宮弘明（そうみや　ひろあき）
1946年名古屋市生まれ、名古屋大学大学院農学研究科博士課程満了。農学博士。
中部大学客員教授（中部高等学術研究所）、中部大学名誉教授、名古屋大学名誉教授。
専門分野：魚類生物学、環境生物学。
共編著：『魚の科学事典』朝倉書店（2005）、共訳書：『生態系サービスという挑戦』名古屋大学出版会（2010）、『樹の力』風媒社（2014）など。

三島浩路（みしま　こうじ）
1962年生まれ。名古屋大学大学院教育発達科学研究科修了、博士（心理学）。中部大学現代教育学部教授。専門分野：社会心理学、学校心理学。
主たる研究領域：児童生徒の「いじめ」やスマートフォン依存に関する調査研究。
論文：「中学生当時のいじめ被害と高校入学後の学校適応との関連」社会心理学研究38 巻（2022）2号、「スマートフォン依存傾向に関連する要因：日常生活に対する主観的評価と自己意識との関連」応用心理学研究46巻（2020）1号など。

中部大学ブックシリーズ　Acta 36

大学の喪失　その再生への期待

詩人ウェンデル・ベリーの教育論

2024 年 3 月 20 日　第 1 刷発行

定　価　（本体 800 円＋税）

著　者　ウェンデル・ベリー

訳　者　鈴木順子　宗宮弘明

発行所　中部大学
〒 487-8501　愛知県春日井市松本町 1200
電　話　0568-51-1111
F A X　0568-51-1141

発　売　風媒社
〒 460-0011 名古屋市中区大須 1-16-29
電　話　052-218-7808
F A X　052-218-7709

ISBN978-4-8331-4162-8